505
FOOTBALL QUESTIONS

YOUR FRIENDS
CAN'T ANSWER

505
FOOTBALL
QUESTIONS

YOUR FRIENDS
CAN'T ANSWER

HAROLD
ROSENTHAL

WALKER AND COMPANY ✺ NEW YORK

796.332
R815f

053596

First published in the United States of America in 1980 by the Walker Publishing Company, Inc.

Published simultaneously in Canada by Beaverbooks, Limited, Don Mills, Ontario.

ISBN 0-8027-0661-4 (cloth); 0-8027-7163-7 (paperback)

Library of Congress Catalog Card Number: 80-51537

Printed in the United States of America

10 9 8 7 6 5 4 3 2 1

ACKNOWLEDGMENT

Many friends and colleagues made considerable contributions to *505 Football Questions Your Friends Can't Answer*. A special thanks is directed toward the two Don Smiths, one from the Pro Football Hall of Fame, the other from Seagram's Seven Crowns of Sport; Steve Boda, Jr., of the National Collegiate Athletic Association; and Jimmie McDowell, of the National Football Foundation Hall of Fame. Ruth Cavin was especially helpful with her editing.

Contents

Introduction

Even if your knowledge of football is limited to the fact that it is a game played with eleven on a side, chances are that you'll score on some of the *505 Football Questions Your Friends Can't Answer.* That's because most Americans have grown up with a certain exposure to the sports pages and headlines; invariably something has penetrated the psyche, to be stored against the day someone asks, "What was Red Grange's number?", and you snap the correct answer, "77".

The correct answers to the 505 questions in this book are something else. If you score in the vicinity of 70 percent, someone ought to give you a free ticket to the next Super Bowl. Anything higher and you should proceed directly to the Hall of Fame, the college pantheon at King's Island, Ohio, or the pros' in Canton, Ohio.

An effort has been made to intermingle what has come to be called "trivia" with the solid information that every football fan, or football fan's wife or girl friend, should know. A recent poll conducted by a completely unreliable survey organization has indicated that "trivia" has become the third most popular American pastime. (The reader is left to figure out the other two.)

Football is an outgrowth of rugby, an English sport, just as baseball is a descendant of "rounders," another English sport. It is for this reason that this Q.-and-A. book, together with its opinions, has been written in English, or a reasonable facsimile. The facts, however, will stand up, even had they been promulgated in Urdu. The author, once a 156-pound high school "running guard" with baby fat to match, has spent all of his life, with the exception of 3½ years in the U.S. Army Air Forces, in pursuit of athletes, athletes' thoughts, and the clever phrasing to describe both. In the course of these activities he has been variously a newspaperman (New York *Herald Trib-*

une) covering all the big showcase sporting events; a football press agent (the Continental League, the American Football League, and the National Football League in that order); an author and collaborator, with his most successful book being a joining of the minds with John Unitas to produce *Playing Pro Football to Win.*

Football has come a long way in the last half century when you realize that it took the pros a dozen years just to figure out that someone should keep records of how many yards a runner gained or how many passes a receiver caught. Colleges were even less conscientious in their record keeping. The game, the fresh air, the pretty girls, and the teary recollections of alma mater were really all that mattered.

For better or worse, that's all been changed. We are now programmed to watch football on the tube until our kidneys ache almost as much as the muscles of the left guard who takes all that illegal buffeting. We argue the merits of the coaching soft-sell compared to the method taskmaster who drives 'em through two-a-day under the 100-degrees July sun. We wait for Super Sunday in late January as though it's the day the lawyer is going to read the family will.

All this, and more, has been taken into consideration in formulating *505 Football Questions Your Friends Can't Answer.* If they all can, go get yourself some different friends. These friends are too, too smart.

FIRST QUARTER

Who Said...?

1. "There is nothing wrong with controlled violence"?

2. "Let 'em go get a football"?

3. "Anyone who says he'd rather dig ditches has never dug ditches"?

4. "They looked like a Chinese fire drill"?

5. "I'm going into the trucking business; there's no future in pro football"?

6. "There hasn't been anything new in football in the last fifty years"?

7. "The older we get the faster we ran as a boy"?

8. "If you cheat, your wives will be the first to know, because I'll tell 'em"?

9. "There isn't a team in the NFL that can make it without TV money"?

10. "Football's a game of blocking and tackling played down in the dirt"?

11. "If he loses a million a year he should be broke in about 150 years"?

12. "There can't be any disrespect where no disrespect is intended"?

13. "I like football because I can do things in it I'd be arrested for on the street"?

ANSWERS

1. *Vince Lombardi, then at the height of his coaching career with the Green Bay Packers. That was a dozen years ago and times have changed. "Violence" is a word soft-pedaled around the NFL, and a strong effort has been made to try to legislate out aspects of the game that make for crippling injuries.*

2. *Bert Bell's advice to the All-America Football Conference in the mid-forties when that rival league was formed in opposition to the NFL, of which Bell was then commissioner. Eventually, the NFL persevered and forced a merger on its own terms. One of the AAFC teams, Paul Brown's Cleveland Browns, came in and dominated the combined league for most of the 1950s.*

3. *When Commissioner Pete Rozelle suspended Joe Namath for refusing to sever his connection with a bar that was under surveillance by Federal agents, Namath's No.-1 receiver on the victorious Super Bowl III Jets team, George Sauer, announced he was quitting, too, saying, "I'd rather dig ditches." Gerry Philbin, a somewhat more realistic defensive end, declared, "Anyone who says he'd 'rather dig ditches' has never dug ditches."*

4. *This was Hank Stram's description of the bewildered condition of the Minnesota Vikings during his Kansas City Chiefs' Super Bowl IV victory over the NFL champions in the last AFL–NFL Super Bowl clash. Stram, an obliging guy, had agreed to be wired for sound for the NFL Films epic of the event. His remark didn't win too many friends for him among the other clubs.*

5. *Pete Rozelle isn't the only man ever to hold the job of Commissioner of the NFL, but has held it the longest. Two commissioners before him, Elmer Layden, one of the Notre Dame Four Horsemen, had the job. In 1946 Layden resigned and took a position in the trucking industry in Chicago, observing that there was no future in pro football.*

6. *Red Grange, the first pro superstar back in the twenties, was interviewed on the occasion of the fiftieth anniversary of his debut in pro football. He said that in all that time he hadn't seen anything new.*

[14]

7. *The Giants had a head coach, Steve Owen, who held the job for more than two decades and produced many winners for the New York club. He got off that line describing the boasting of an old ball player against whom he had played in the pioneer days.*

8. *Most training camps are either loose-as-a-goose or as tight as discipline on a naval destroyer. In the latter category are the Cincinnati Bengals, where Paul Brown, former head coach, is still very much the boss in a front-office capacity. Brown used to address the troops on the first day of training camp. Philandering by his married players was high on the list of taboos.*

9. *Thursday night games, 5:30 starting times on the West Coast (to get the prime-time network viewers back East), and other tidbits have made television the tail that wags the pro football dog. (Since this results in approximately $5 million per club in the safe before the season opens, most people would be willing to submit to a lot of that kind of tail-wagging). Commissioner Pete Rozelle, who led pro football into this financial bonanza, realized the route he was taking ten years ago. In a formal press conference in 1971 he was asked how many teams in the NFL could make it without TV. "Zilch," said Pete.*

10. *Vince Lombardi's back again, with the line about "rock-'em, sock-'em." He wasn't just humming a tune, Vince wasn't, because he was one of Fordham University's famed Seven Blocks of Granite back in the thirties and took a lot of punishment as a 180-pound guard in college. He never got beyond the minor league level in the pros, playing with the Wilmington Bombers in the American Association.*

11. *Lamar Hunt is the son of the late H.L. Hunt, one of the biggest oil wildcatters and sports gamblers in history. Hunt was still in his twenties when he helped form the American Football League as a rival of the NFL in 1960. He lost a potful of money that first season—maybe a million—bucking the Dallas Cowboys with a rival team in his home town. When his father heard about it, he shrugged and said, "Well at that rate he's got another 150 years to go," or words to that effect. H.L. then got back to the business of making quarter-million dollar bets on college football while munching on the sandwich he had carried from home in a brown paper bag.*

12. *The weekend after John F. Kennedy was assassinated, the NFL had to make a big decision on whether or not to play before the president was even buried. The American Football League called off their games but the NFL decided to go on with theirs, ordering that all the fancy business with bands, cheerleaders, etc. be dispensed with. A number of important sportswriters called the fledgling commissioner on it, questioning his judgment and implying that he was showing disrespect for a slain president. Pete Rozelle then offered his comment about "disrespect". Years later he said that if he had a chance to do it again his choice would have been a different one.*

13. *Mike (The Animal) Curtis, NFL linebacker who played for more than a decade and a half.*

Didn't You Used to Be...?

Football is no more immune to change than any other aspect of the American scene. Clubs come, leagues go, indispensable players of a half-dozen years ago have to pay their way into the park today. The only thing to be counted upon is that somewhere today there is a youth who will be tomorrow's hero, and his name will sound as though we have heard it all our lives.

It's that way with clubs, too. Philadelphia Eagles, Detroit Lions, San Diego Chargers, Kansas City Chiefs—they've been around forever, right? Wrong.

Try matching some of these current clubs with their predecessors, ranging from the days when fifty dollars a game was a good day's pay to the early sixties as the American Football League was backing and filling for its ten-year drive toward eventual merger with the older NFL.

1. The Philadelphia Eagles were preceded by a club that played in a nearby suburb. What was the name of that club?

2. The Detroit Lions play their games in the Silverdome in Pontiac, Michigan, though they still carry the Detroit tag. Who were they before they became the Lions?

3. In 1925 the NFL title was given to the Chicago Cardinals. The real winner played a Notre Dame All-Star team post-season and disqualified itself. What was the name of the first winning team, and what was the reason for its disqualification?

4. George Marshall's Redskins won the 1936 Eastern Division title, but the championship game with Green Bay was

[17]

played away from either team's city. (The Redskins lost, 21–0.) What was the reason for the switch? (For the same reason, Marshall's team got a new name the following year.)

5. The New York Jets had a former name that was connected with the last club insolvency in the history of the National or American Football Leagues. What was the name, and what was unusual about its owner?

6. The Chicago Bears have more Hall of Fame occupants than any other club in the pantheon in Canton. What was the name they started under, and why the switch to the Bears?

ANSWERS

1. *The Eagles' predecessor was the Frankford Yellow Jackets. This team was available for play every day except Sunday because of the "blue laws" then prevalent in Pennsylvania.*

2. *The Detroit Lions started life as the Portsmouth Spartans in that section of Ohio which proved the No.-1 hotbed of the burgeoning pro game. Paydays were few and far between for the Spartans, even though they were a championship contender, until a radio man bought the club and moved it to Detroit.*

3. *The only club ever to win an NFL championship and have it taken away again was the Pottsville (Pa.) Maroons, a tough bunch from the coal-mining section of eastern Pennsylvania in the mid-twenties. There was no play-off in those days, and Pottsville finished with the best record in the league. They had a chance for some good money in a game against the Notre Dame All-Stars in Philadelphia and they took it. Notre Dame was considered the No.-1 college team in the country. The aforementioned Frankford Yellow Jackets screamed bloody murder about its territorial rights being violated by another member of the league. The league president out in Dayton decided in their favor, took away the championship, and awarded it to the next-best club, the Chicago Cardinals. Pottsville has been trying to get the title back ever since. In three subsequent wars its sons have carried the story to the far ends of the earth.*

4. *The Washington Redskins started life as the Boston Redskins and lasted two seasons in Beantown. When it was obvious to George Marshall, then owner, that he was never going to make it there, he moved the site of the season's-end championship game with Green Bay to the Polo Grounds, where it managed to draw decently. The following year Marshall moved the club to Washington, where he ran a wet-wash business. There the team was an immediate success, attracting Washington fans to its games in droves and pulling 10,000 of them to its contests with the Giants in New York.*

5. *The New York Jets started as the New York Titans when the AFL was formed in 1960. It was a rag-tag outfit, traveling economy and ducking hotel bills largely because its owner, Harry Wismer, had suffered reverses in the stock market and was undercapitalized.*

[19]

He finally went bust in 1962 and the season finished with the League paying the players' salaries. Then a new crowd came in, renamed the team the Jets, and it went out to a Super Bowl triumph.

Wismer was a dandy. He had been a successful radio announcer and had owned a piece of the Washington Redskins. His idea of advance promotion when his team played on the road was to send along one hundred photos—all of himself.

6. *The Chicago Bears started life as the Decatur Staleys in downstate Illinois. George Halas got jobs for his players with the Staley Starch Company, whose owner firmly believed that football, pro football, was the game of the future. After a year the cost of operating the club was too much for the company and the owner gave the whole operation to Halas, who took it to Chicago, his hometown, where he made a good deal with the baseball club that owned Wrigley Field (and still does). Since the ball club was known as the Cubs, Halas felt the least he could do was to call his club the Bears.*

And Then There Are the Smiths

"Smith" is the most popular name in the United States and has been for a long time. There are four in the College Football Hall of Fame but none in the Pro. Closest to "Smith" in the Pros is Joe Schmidt, the Detroit linebacker and former Lions coach. There have been big Smiths like Billy Ray, the Colts' defensive tackle, and little Smiths like Noland, who measured 5'6" when he played for the Kansas City Chiefs and had to wear a single digit (1) on the back of his shirt because he wasn't wide enough to spread out a couple of numbers.

1. Who are the Smiths in the National Football Foundation's Hall of Fame in King's Island, Ohio?

2. Why are the names Bubba and Tody Smith linked?

3. What Smith played longest in the pros?

4. Which Smiths have coached successfully?

5. As long as we're talking about Bubba and Tody Smith, what were their real names?

6. What Smith, who starred in the NFL, was called by his initials only?

7. What Smith played pro, than went on to become sports editor for one of the nation's great newspapers?

8. Were there more John Smiths playing pro football than any other brand of Smith?

9. Which Smith was a Heisman Trophy winner?

[21]

ANSWERS

1. *Bruce (Boo) Smith, Minnesota halfback; Ernie Smith, Southern California tackle; Harry (Blackjack) Smith, Southern California guard; and John (Clipper) Smith, Notre Dame guard, are the Smiths in the College Hall of Fame.*

2. *Bubba and Tody Smith, brothers, were NFL defensive linemen, Bubba with the Baltimore Colts, Tody with the Cowboys. Bubba was the better player, but his career was cut short when he ran into a linesman's measuring pole during an exhibition game.*

3. *Jackie Smith, a tight end from Northwest Louisiana, played in the big leagues from 1963 through 1979, finishing up with the Cowboys after a long career with the St. Louis Cardinals, where he set all their receiving records. He is twelfth among the all-time receivers with 480 catches.*

4. *Andy Smith, who coached the University of California "Wonder Teams" a half century ago, was the leading Smith in the coaching fraternity. He also coached at Penn and Purdue. Carnie Smith coached Pittsburg State to two NAIA championships. Blackjack Smith was head coach of the Saskatchewan Roughriders in the Canadian League in the early fifties.*

5. *Bubba Smith's real name was Charles, and Tody's was Lawrence. When Bubba was at Michigan State, the terrifying chant from the Spartans' adherents was "Kill, Bubba," which was a lot more frightening than "Kill, Charles" would have been.*

6. *J.D. Smith was a 1,000-yard runner for the 49ers in that backfield which included Hugh McElhenny. He roomed with R.C. Owens, who also went by initials only. R.C. was also known as "Alley-Oop," a tribute to his ability to out jump everyone on defense.*

7. *Wilfred Smith was a pro pioneer after coming out of DePauw University. He played end for the Hammond Pros, the Louisville Brecks, and the Chicago Cardinals; and when he finished, he climbed into the press box. Ultimately, he became sports editor for the* Chicago Tribune.

[22]

8. *Surprisingly, only three John Smiths have played in pros, compared to a half-dozen Jim Smiths. There have been no John Does.*

9. *The Heisman-winning Smith was Bruce Smith, Minnesota running back, who won in 1941. He was also team captain when the Gophers had a seventeen-game winning streak and won the national title two straight years. He played for Green Bay and the Los Angeles Rams.*

Will the 1,000-Yard Club Please Come to Order?

The origin of the 1,000-Yard Club in pro football is a little vague. A number of people have attemped to take credit, the writer included. Up to the 1960s, fewer than three dozen runners in both the NFL and AFL had accomplished this feat. Every one of them seemed to be named either Jim Brown or Jim Taylor.

The increase in the number of games played, from twelve to fourteen, then to sixteen, has caused the list to burgeon. With approximately twenty new names being added each season these days, club membership is going to lose a lot of its gloss. There are, however, some great names on it, and it's certainly worthy of study.

In the event some authentic atmosphere is desired while attempting to answer the questions, the test may be taken in the actual 1,000-Yard Club, a cocktail joint in Appleton, Wisconsin, run by Fuzzy Thurston, the old Green Bay lineman, who figured he knew enough 1,000-yard runners in his day to name his place in their honor.

1. Who holds the record for the greatest number of 1,000-yard seasons, of course, of course?

2. O.J. Simpson holds the all-time record of 2,003, set with

[24]

Buffalo in 1973. How many times has he gone over 1,000 yards?

3. Who was the first 1,000-yard runner, and how many games did he require?

4. Who was the first rookie to make 1,000?

5. Who were the 1,000-yard runners to hit it right on the nose?

6. Who was the shortest 1,000-yard runner?

7. Among the top fifteen performances of 1,000 yards or more, who leads?

8. Has any runner ever put together two 1,000-yard efforts in his first two years?

9. What was the unusual facet of Spec Sanders's 1,000 season with the N.Y. Yankees in the All-America Conference in 1947?

10. The NFL picked the all-time team on the occasion of its fiftieth anniversary at the start of the seventies. Which of the three runners never achieved 1,000 yards in a season?

11. Jim Brown played in the NFL for nine years before moving to a movie career. Did he ever have a non-1,000-yards season?

12. When O.J. Simpson rushed for that 2,003 yards, topping 2,000 in his last game of the season, whose previous all-time record did he break?

ANSWERS

1. *Surprise. As of the 1980 season, that honor was shared by Franco Harris, of the Pittsburgh Steelers, and Jim Brown, of the Cleveland Browns, each with seven. Purists might suggest that Brown's effort was more meritorious. He performed in an era that began with a twelve-game season and went to fourteen. Franco came in when fourteen games were scheduled, and in 1978 and 1979 he had the benefit of the sixteen-game season. In fairness to Franco, however, he never asked anyone to increase the number to sixteen games.*

2. *O.J. did it five times and was unlucky. He began under a Buffalo coach who was reluctant to use him as his leading offensive weapon, and he finished his career playing hurt, off and on, during his last three seasons.*

3. *The first man to break 1,000 was Beattie Feathers, in 1934 with the Chicago Bears. He missed one game with an injury but racked up 1,004 yards on only 101 carries for an amazing 9.9 yards per carry. Half that average is considered a top-drawer effort.*

4. *Feathers was also the first rookie to do it. He had help. He operated in the same backfield as Bronko Nagurski, the Hall of Fame fullback who ran interference.*

5. *Those who achieved 1,000 smack on the nose were Willie Ellison, Los Angeles, 1971; Mercury Morris, Miami, 1972; and Greg Pruitt, Cleveland, 1976.*

6. *Shortest 1,000-yard runner was Charlie Tolar, listed at 5'6" on the Houston Oilers roster. He looked shorter, and he was used mainly for hitting inside.*

7. *Among the top fifteen performances, Jim Brown's name appears four times, O.J. Simpson's three. Walt Payton, of the Chicago Bears, and Earl Campbell are in there twice.*

8. *Earl Campbell, of Houston, had 1,450 yards his first year, 1,697 his second. No man ever had 3,000 yards in his first two years.*

9. *Orban (Spec) Sanders was the triple threat in the old single-wing offense used by the Yankees in the All-America Conference.*

He was the club's leading passer and punter when he ran for 1,432 yards in 1947. A knee injury diminished his effectiveness but he returned to lead the league in interceptions as a defensive back.

10. *On the NFL's all-time team Jim Brown was the fullback and Gale Sayers and Hugh McElhenny were the halfbacks. McElhenny never hit 1,000 although he topped 900 in 1956.*

11. *Jim Brown missed 1,000 in two of his seasons, in 1957, his first and then in 1962 a couple of years before he finished. In both cases he bettered 900 yards.*

12. *Before O.J. Simpson broke 2,000 for a season, the record was 1,863 set by Jim Brown in 1963.*

The "First American" Athlete

In 1950 the Associated Press signaled the completion of a half century with a national media poll on the greatest figures in sports during those fifty years. Jim Thorpe won highest honors, both as the top football player and as the outstanding male athlete, beating such superstars as Babe Ruth, Jack Dempsey, Bill Tilden, Bobby Jones and Man o' War. Thorpe realized comparatively little materially from his athletic ability and died a few years after being voted this highest honor.

An additional three decades has failed to diminish the glamour surrounding this great athlete's name. There are almost as many Thorpe stories around as those about Dempsey and Ruth. Brushing up on his background:

1. Thorpe was a full-blooded Indian. What was his tribe?

2. What was the Indian school he attended?

3. On the team that played the top college teams of the era, there was another native American, a halfback named Joe Guyon, who is in the Pro Hall of Fame along with Thorpe. What was Guyon's tribe?

4. Thorpe has a town in Pennsylvania named after him—Jim Thorpe, Pa. What had been its former name?

5. Thorpe played for a half-dozen NFL clubs. Two of them adopted the nickname "Indians". What were these two clubs?

6. With the New York Giants, on the down side of his pro career, Thorpe had a very special salary arrangement. What was it?

7. Thorpe won two gold medals in the 1912 Olympic games in Stockholm, then was disqualified when it became known he had played minor league baseball in North Carolina, and his medals were taken from him. What were the two events he won?

8. Were the medals ever returned to him?

9. What position did Thorpe hold on the administrative side of sports?

ANSWERS

1. *Thorpe was a member of the Sac and Fox tribe. His grand-father was a Black Hawk war chief.*

2. *Thorpe attended the Carlisle (Pa.) Indian School where the coach was Glenn S. (Pop) Warner, one of the game's great in-novators.*

3. *Guyon was a Chippewa who blocked for Thorpe, later was an All-America at Georgia Tech. He was, like Thorpe, a superb kicker and his 95-yard record, set in 1920, remained in the book for fifty years.*

4. *In an effort to get on the map by setting up a shrine to Thorpe, the town of Mauch Chunk, Pa., changed its name officially a decade ago. It was supposed to attract tourists, funds for a big hospital, etc. It didn't help but the place is still "Jim Thorpe." (It has a nicer sound than "Mauch Chunk".)*

5. *Among the NFL clubs Thorpe played for in the league's first decade were the Cleveland Indians and the Oorang Indians. "Oorang" was neither a city nor a tribe but the name of a kennel operation in Marion, Ohio. In those days the NFL took its bidders for franchises where they could find them.*

6. *Thorpe had one season with the New York Giants and by that time was pretty well used up. He was still better paid than the rest, but the arrangement was that he would be paid by the half. If he couldn't come up for the second half, he got only fifty percent of what was due him.*

7. *Thorpe won the pentathlon (five events) and the decathlon (ten events) at the 1912 Olympics in Stockholm. It is a double that can never be equaled because the pentathlon was dropped after the 1924 Olympics.*

8. *The medals were never returned despite all sorts of efforts by Congress and other interested parties. However, in 1973 the AAU restored Thorpe's amateur standing posthumously.*

9. When they formed the first pro league in 1920, it was called the American Professional Football Association and they got Thorpe to serve as president in order to capitalize on his name. He and the Association lasted one year. The following season it became the National Football League and a midwestern promoter, Joe Carr, took over and ran it for a couple of decades.

SECOND QUARTER

The Establishment

1. In 1920 the organizational meeting for the NFL was held in Ralph Hay's automobile agency in Canton, Ohio. What kind of car did he handle?

2. How much did the first franchises cost in the NFL?

3. The Columbus Panhandles were early members of the League. How was this club different from the rest of the teams?

4. What was the amount involved in the first player deal in the NFL?

5. In the sixties "Packer" came to be synonymous with power. Where did the nickname "Packers" come from for the Green Bay team?

6. Tim Mara bought a franchise for New York as a kind of afterthought. What had been his original intention that day?

7. What was the first play-off in NFL history?

8. In what year was the passing rule changed so that a pass could be made from anywhere behind the line of scrimmage rather than from 5 yards behind?

9. What was the first rival league to challenge the NFL?

10. In 1946 the All-America Conference set up as another rival for the NFL, posing a threat many times greater; it was coast to coast and had substantial backing in most of its cities. Jonas Ingram was its first commissioner. What was unusual about him?

11. When the All-America Conference folded in '49, what clubs were absorbed into the NFL?

12. What was the first NFL club to have all its games televised?

13. What was the first game televised from coast to coast?

14. What was the last pro team to abandon the single-wing formation with the ball handler getting a direct snap from center?

ANSWERS

1. *Hay handled Hupmobile. The founding fathers sat around that day on the running boards of the cars for the most part. There weren't enough seats.*

2. *Franchises in the beginning cost one hundred dollars, and there is no record of anyone having sent his check to cover.*

3. *The Columbus Panhandles offered six Nesser brothers in various positions, making it a little difficult for a hot-headed rival to lose his temper and question the ancestry of someone playing opposite him. The last Nesser, Al, a guard, lasted until 1932 with Green Bay.*

4. *Bob Nash was the first player to figure in a deal. Akron sold him to Buffalo for $300 and 5 percent of the gate receipts. Nash was a lineman.*

5. *The Packers were originally sponsored by a Green Bay meat-packing company.*

6. *When Tim Mara bought a franchise in the NFL for New York ("a franchise for anything in New York should be worth $500"), he had dropped in on a fight manager looking to buy an interest in the contract of Gene Tunney.*

7. *The first play-off came in 1932 between the Bears and Portsmouth (later Detroit) when both finished with six victories and one defeat. The game was moved indoors when a blizzard hit Chicago, and the Bears won 9-0, with the Spartans complaining that Bronko Nagurski had thrown an illegal pass to Red Grange for the touchdown.*

8. *The pass rule was changed for the 1934 season.*

9. *In 1926 Red Grange's manager was turned down by George Halas in his request for a salary in five figures and a third interest in the Bears, so he started his own league, making Grange the centerpiece of a team in New York called the Yankees and playing in Yankee Stadium. It lasted a single season.*

10. *In 1946 the All-America Conference brought pro ball to San*

Francisco, Cleveland, Baltimore, and Buffalo, as well as putting rival clubs in New York, Los Angeles, and Chicago. For its top man it picked Admiral Jonas Ingram, former commander of the Atlantic frontier during World War II and an outstanding college player in his Naval Academy days.

11. In 1950, Cleveland, San Francisco, and Baltimore were absorbed into the NFL after the AAFC folded. They matched the NFL championship Philadelphia team with Cleveland in the season opener to teach the newcomers a lesson—and Cleveland beat the Eagles badly.

12. The Los Angeles Rams made a deal with the Admiral TV people to permit all their games to be televised, with the stipulation that any loss in revenue, as calculated by any drop in attendance from the previous year, would be made up by the sponsors. It cost Admiral more than $300,000 for the 1950 experiment.

13. In 1951 the Cleveland–Los Angeles championship game was telecast from coast to coast. The DuMont Network paid $75,000 for the rights. That would buy about a snappy 5-second commercial on today's Super Bowl telecast.

14. Pittsburgh was the last NFL team to let go of the single-wing, switching to the T-formation in 1952.

Nicknames

The informality of sports makes nicknames an integral part of football. It is also a good way to shake a name that has nagged you ever since you got stuck with it to please a doting aunt. Here are a handful of the best-known ones that have graced the gridiron. The first one is tough, but after that it's comparatively downhill for those who have followed the game with any degree of attention. How many real first names can you supply?

1. Afterburner Atkins
2. Sam Baker
3. Red Blaik
4. Rocky Bleier
5. Dutch Clark
6. Buddy Dial
7. Paddy Driscoll
8. Speedy Duncan
9. Turk Edwards
10. Weeb Ewbank
11. Chuck Forman
12. Frenchy Fuqua
13. Cookie Gilchrist
14. Jug Girard
15. Goose Gonsoulin
16. Red Grange
17. Fats Henry
18. Crazy Legs Hirsch
19. Hunchy Hoernschmeyer
20. Chick Jagade
21. Dub Jones
22. Special Delivery Jones
23. Sonny Jurgensen
24. Shipwreck Kelly

25. Bruiser Kinard
26. Curly Lambeau
27. Night Train Lane
28. TuffyLeemans
29. Big Daddy Lipscomb
30. Spider Lockhart
31. Link Lyman
32. Pug Manders
33. Tuss McLaughry
34. Mercury Morris
35. Bronko Nagurski
36. Greasy Neale
37. Babe Parilli
38. Ace Parker
39. Joe Perry
40. Sonny Randle
41. Spec Sanders
42. Vitamin Smith
43. Bart Starr
44. Fuzzy Thurston
45. Bulldog Turner
46. Whizzer White
47. Buddy Young
48. Waddy Young
49. Tank Younger

ANSWERS

1. *Pervis Atkins*
2. *Loris Baker*
3. *Earl Blaik*
4. *Robert Bleier*
5. *Earl Clark*
6. *Gilbert Dial*
7. *John Driscoll*
8. *Leslie Duncan*
9. *Glen Edwards*
10. *Wilber Ewbank*
11. *Walter Forman*
12. *John Fuqua*
13. *Carleton Gilchrist*
14. *Earl Girard*
15. *Austin Gonsoulin*
16. *Harold Grange*
17. *Wilbur Henry*
18. *Elroy Hirsch*
19. *Bob Hoernschmeyer*
20. *Harry Jagade*
21. *Bill Jones*
22. *Edgar Jones*
23. *Christian Jurgensen*
24. *John Kelly*
25. *Frank Kinard*
26. *Earl Lambeau*
27. *Dick Lane*
28. *Alphonse Leemans*
29. *Gene Lipscomb*
30. *Carl Lockhart*
31. *Roy Lyman*
32. *Clarence Manders*
33. *DeOrmond McLaughry*
34. *Gene Morris*
35. *Bronislaw Nagurski*
36. *Earle Neale*
37. *Vito Parilli*

38. *Clarence Parker*
39. *Fletcher Perry*
40. *Ulmo Randle*
41. *Orban Sanders*
42. *Verda Smith*
43. *Bryan Starr*
44. *Fred Thurston*
45. *Clyde Turner*
46. *Byron White*
47. *Claude Young*
48. *Walter Young*
49. *Paul Younger*

Darling, They're Speaking Our Language

Borrowing from every section of the country and putting together the speech patterns of dozens of different callings, football has developed a patois that frequently sounds like gibberish to the outsider. Yet it is one of the most effective of spoken shorthands, and provides a link between the millions who follow the game and those who play and direct.

Other sectors, including the military and industry, have dipped into football's ample bag and put its words and phrases to their own particular use ("game plan," "mousetrap," "prevent defense," "hearing footsteps," are only a few that have burgeoned into general use).

Let us also not forget the "Monday morning quarterback," the "cheap shot," and the "double-teaming," which need no explanation to the vast majority of listeners. And we all know we're in trouble when the six-year-old refuses to play with the kid next door, not because he's a "show-off" but because he's a "hot dog."

Here are some of the more widely used items in football's *lingua franca*. If you know ninety percent of their meanings, drop whatever you're doing and pick up a helmet.

1. Alley oop
2. Audible
3. Bootleg
4. Coffin corner

5. Cab squad
6. Catch-up
7. Cheap shot
8. Cliff-hanger
9. Clothesline
10. Crackback
11. Don't hit him, he's dead
12. Double-team
13. Eat the ball
14. Fire out
15. Flea-flicker
16. Footsteps
17. Forearm shiver
18. Front four
19. Game plan
20. The hammer
21. Head-hunter
22. Hot dog
23. Knee
24. Looping
25. Meat grinder
26. Monday morning quarterback
27. Mousetrap
28. Nutcracker
29. The pit
30. The pocket
31. Prevent defense
32. Quick-whistle
33. Red dog, blitz, shoot the gap
34. Ring bell
35. Short stuff
36. Shotgun
37. Skull session
38. Sleeper
39. Special teams

ANSWERS

1. *Alley oop: A long forward pass, thrown up for grabs, usually in desperation. It goes back to circus lingo where the aerialists would shout "alley-oop!", boosting a member of the troupe to the topmost point of a human pyramid. In football the intended recipient is usually a sprinter who doesn't bother with guile or deception but races for the end zone, hoping to reach it ahead of the defenders and at approximately the same time as the ball.*

2. *Audible: A quarterback calls the play in a huddle and the subsequent signals tell when the action will begin. Sometimes as the players line up he'll note that the play is doomed for any of several reasons, including that the opposition has guessed what he intends to do and has lined up accordingly. In this case he'll call a specially designated number which means that the play is canceled and another has replaced it. All this is split-second stuff. Enough audibles in a particular season will cause even the most erudite lineman to wonder whether he shouldn't go into the family blacksmithing business.*

3. *Bootleg: This is an instance where the most valuable piece of bric-a-brac on the field, the quarterback, risks life and limb by keeping the ball on a running play. He conceals it against his leg as best he can, starts running, all the while looking for a soft spot on which to fall just before the mammoths hit him.*

4. *Coffin corner: To do with kickers rather than undertakers. The idea in punting is to put the ball as close to the opponent's goal line as possible without its going over, which would mean they take possession on their own 20. Instead the punter tries to make the kick go out "on the 2" (the 2-yard line), which is called the "coffin corner". Some people make an excellent living in pro ball for years with this talent, and never even get a grass stain on their uniform.*

5. *Cab squad: This is the group of players who didn't make the club after training camp for one reason or another. A club is permitted "x"number of players on its cab squad, and a certain amount of mobility in moving them onto the regular team. "Cab" goes back to the days of the Cleveland Browns in the late forties when they were owned by a taxi mogul named Mickey McBride. When a player was* *cut, he wasn't sent packing but was given a job driving one of McBride's cabs.*

6. *Catch-up: Used mostly as an adjective, as in "to play 'catch-up' ball". You fall behind and you're battling two factors, the other team and the clock, so you resort to tactics that will get you back into the game in a hurry. You pass. This is known as "playing catch-up." It puts the quarterback under tremendous pressure because everyone in the park knows he's going to pass and acts accordingly.*

7. *Cheap shot: Anyone running with the ball, or trying to catch it, is obviously at a disadvantage in protecting his various anatomical portions. The runner has to use one arm to hang onto the ball; the receiver has to leap and leave unprotected his rib cage and kidney area. There are legal ways of sticking a helmet in there without breaking the rules. There are also instances of a "late hit," where the player is down and the defender, apparently unable to halt his own momentum, delivers a final damaging blow. Some players develop this ability to a high level of perfection and win the title of "cheap shot artist." Their defense is that "It's football, not ballet."*

8. *Cliff-hanger: Football here has gone to the old dime serial movies for this one, meaning something that isn't decided until the last few seconds. In the old movies the hero (or heroine) would be left hanging from a tree root on the side of a cliff, and you'd be left to wonder an entire week whether the victim would be rescued in the next episode. He (or she) was.*

9. *Clothesline: This is like running into a clothesline in the dark. It catches you up under the chin, and if you live you do it eating soft foods for the next couple of weeks. Only here the defender's level arm takes the place of the clothesline. All very legal.*

10. *Crackback: This is a type of block in which the wide receivers and flankers start out as if they are going to run a pass pattern, then suddenly block the linebackers nearest them. They sort of "crack back," and the element of surprise is essential. If it's lacking, the "crackers," outweighed by thirty or forty pounds, wind up victims of the "crackees."*

11. *Don't hit him, he's dead: Inside lingo used by the referee whose principal job, once the offensive play is in motion, is to pro-*

tect the quarterback. Once the quarterback gets rid of the ball he is no longer a target. He's out of the play, dead, hence the referee's shouted admonition to some onrushing human steamroller.

12. *Double-team: Sometimes it's necessary to put two men on the job of containing one exceptional performer, therefore the expression, which means a team effort. If you double-team you leave another area unprotected. The idea is to use deception if you have to do it through the whole game. If you do, the defense will invariably make a costly mistake.*

13. *Eat the ball: There comes a time when a quarterback realizes that whatever he does will be canceled out effectively by the opposition. And if he tries to throw the ball it'll probably mean an interception. So he retains it, gathering it into the vicinity of his sternum for maximum protection. This is known as "eating the ball," which is of course a figure of speech unless you have the jaw capacity of a boa constrictor.*

14. *Fire out: A maneuver by the offensive linemen, a fast take-off from their position, usually dead-ahead.*

15. *Flea-flicker: Description of a multistage pass play, usually a forward with an ensuing lateral tacked on. It goes back to Bob Zuppke at Illinois more than a half-century ago, and it's been refined by the pros. Not too many flea-flickers, however, are used in a game because they depend largely upon the element of surprise. The maneuver where a quarterback laterals off to another back, who returns it to the quarterback, who passes it downfield in orthodox fashion, is another version.*

16. *Footsteps: Football players are supposed to be unafraid. Anyone who is rated as less than courageous, particularly receivers who worry about possible damaging effects from the defense as they reach for a pass, are said to be "hearing footsteps".*

17. *Forearm shiver: A move by defensive linemen against onrushing opposition. You bring your forearm up like a club; when it connects properly, the recipient "shivers".*

18. *Front four: Description of the defensive linemen as they line up . . . end, tackle, tackle, end. Sometimes a fifth man, a linebacker, is inserted, and sometimes only three men are used up* *front, permitting the use of four linebackers in a more flexible defense against the pass.*

19. *Game plan: You figure what you can do best and what the opposition can do best. Then your staff helps draw up your "game plan". You stick with this, until you're chased out of it by developments. Overuse has dimmed the phrase's glamour. You have youngsters going out on a Saturday night date asking each other what the game plan is, and presidents announcing that they've come up with a new game plan to straighten everything out, from a fifty-billion dollar deficit to your kid's teeth.*

20. *The hammer: Description of a defending back unloading on a receiver, making certain he remembers the occasion so he will take his business elsewhere on future plays. It comes at a juncture in a passing play where the receiver and the defender have equal rights to the ball.*

21. *Head-hunter: In football this isn't someone who takes your head as a rightful prize in combat and shrinks it to store in his trophy case. It's someone who tackles almost exclusively from the neck up. It's a very effective type of tackling, discouraging the ballcarriers from future efforts. The risk is that an agile runner or quarterback can occasionally slip away and leave the would-be tackler with an awkwardly crocked elbow and nothing else.*

22. *Hot dog: Term used for a show-off, exhibitionist, and look-at-me kind of person. The NFL has tried its best to discourage this type of performance. If you throw a ball into the stands or even bounce one, following a touchdown, it's an automatic $200 fine. Before everyone started to wear 'em, white shoes on the ball field were a sign of a hot dog.*

23. *Knee: That vital portion of the underpinning that plays such an important part in the injury report. It's been abbreviated to the point where the expression, "he has a knee," conveys the information that the player has been injured in that area.*

24. *Looping: A maneuver by defensive linemen to befuddle the opposition's linemen and mix them up in their pass-blocking assignments. Also known as "stunting". This requires good personnel. You can get burned using people of lesser caliber.*

25. *Meat grinder: That area of the opposition's massed strength* *where there is the greatest risk of injury. A tough lineman on offense, carrying out a difficult assignment, is said to be "sticking his head into the meat-grinder."*

26. *Monday morning quarterback: This goes back to Saturday college games, when the customers couldn't wait for Sunday to be over so they could get together and pick things apart on Monday morning. Since pro games are played on Sunday, they don't have to wait that long anymore.*

27. *Mousetrap: This bears a direct relationship to those things you bait and set to get rid of unwelcome little visitors. You set the trap by making it appear as though your offense has made a mistake and left an opening for a defending player to come through and nail your quarterback. The opposing player takes the bait and bang—an offensive lineman, running low and parallel to the line of scrimmage, comes up to flatten him. Then the ballcarrier goes sailing through the hole he has left. You can't do it with defending linemen who sit back and wait; but then again, if they sit back and wait they won't be in there too long.*

28. *Nutcracker: Tchaikovsky gave this name to one of his more famous pieces of music, but in football it's a bone-testing drill used to separate men from callow youths. An offensive and defensive lineman face each other, and there's a running back behind the offensive man. The defender fights off the block and then must tackle the back who tries to race past, within an area restricted by two dummies ten feet apart. This little caper is restricted to training camp and they don't take too many films of it.*

29. *The Pit: Where the offensive and defensive linemen clash head-on. It's the kind of thing described by Upton Sinclair in his early writing about the Chicago stockyards.*

30. *The Pocket: When the quarterback fades back seven or eight paces to pass, he theoretically has immunity from harm for a few seconds because of the alignment of the defenders. The area he occupies is known as "the pocket," and some quarterbacks have managed to spend a successful career in the pocket. The quarterback has to be able to get the ball off, however, because linemen can hold their blocks only so long before the pocket collapses. The intent of the defense is to chase the quarterback out of the pocket and into the open where he should be a prime target because of his* *inability to run and to take general punishment like a running back. Unless he happens to be a Fran Tarkenton.*

31. *Prevent defense: A comparatively new term in football signifying an alignment aimed at stopping the big play that would tie the game or win it in the late going. This usually calls for a fifth defensive back at the expense of a lineman, thereby giving up much of the effectiveness of a pass rush on the quarterback. In a prevent defense you usually concede those short look-in passes. The theory is that time will take care of things, particularly if the other team is deep in its own territory and needs a touchdown. There are coaches, however, who avoid prevent defense on the theory that if you've been winning with one style of play, stick with it. The prevent defense is also called the "nickel defense," "nickel" for that fifth defensive back.*

32. *Quick-whistle: This means that in someone's opinion, usually slanted, the whistle ending the play has been blown too quickly. Big area of dispute here is whether a receiver catching and dropping the ball has retained it long enough to have it ruled a fumble.*

33. *Red dog, blitz, shoot the gap: These are various terms for a defensive player, other than a lineman, leaving his position before the snap in anticipation of a play. If he guesses right he can usually nail the quarterback dead in his tracks because there are no blocking plans on a man moving at the time the ball is snapped. If he guesses wrong he leaves his area naked and usually it means heavy yardage. Never show ignorance by referring to "blitzing linemen". If they leave their positions before the ball is snapped it means a 5-yard penalty.*

34. *Ring bell: A reference here to a legal blow to the helmet vigorous enough to cause the recipient to "hear bells." The usual line is "he rang his bell". An on-rushing defensive lineman, catching his opponent with that one shot permitted, will ring his opponent's bell. Actually, if you hear bells ringing you're well along the path toward a possible concussion..*

35. *Short stuff: The nickel-and-dime passes usually permitted a quarterback by a defense that is ahead and that is largely concerned with preventing the long, successful scoring pass.*

36. *Shotgun: The offensive formation where the quarterback* moves 7 or 8 yards back and takes the direct snap from center. This provides him with an extra half-second for spotting receivers. But at the same time it's a giveaway that he's going to pass. The most successful exponent in pro history of this maneuver has been Roger Staubach with the Dallas Cowboys. He pulled them out of a lot of tight spots with the shotgun.

37. *Skull session:* An analysis of plays and strategy usually participated in by an entire squad. The "skull" means head work is the No. 1 factor here, although some coaches feel other parts of the anatomy are equally as important. One famous line is "The brain can absorb only what the seat can endure."

38. *Sleeper:* A player who drifts inconspicuously out of the general area of play without going offsides and is next seen catching a decisive pass.

39. *Special teams:* Something you work up from, to become a member of either the offense or defense. Special teams are used for kicking plays, offensively and defensively. The reserves get to see action a lot here. No sense having a fragile wide receiver sticking his head into the meat-grinder on a kickoff, unless he is your third or fourth wide receiver.

Was There Ever A College Team That...?

College football predates the pro variety by a half century, so people have been asking questions and seeking answers about the collegiate game that much longer. As soon as one generation gets through with the questions and answers, the next one picks up. Here are fifty of the most frequently asked questions, as collected by the National Collegiate Athletic Association, the body governing major college football (and minor, too). These are NOT necessarily listed in their order of frequency.

1. Name the members of Notre Dame's famed Four Horsemen backfield of 1924.

2. What coach won the most games at one college?

3. Which Rose Bowl game was not played at Pasadena?

4. What team defeated another 222–0?

5. What team played in three different postseason Bowl games the same year?

6. Which team went undefeated during sixty-three games?

7. What coach won the national championship in his first year as a head coach?

8. Which college team has won the most games through the end of 1979 and how many?

9. What teams played in the first intercollegiate football game?

10. What major college team was the last to go through the regular season undefeated, untied, and unscored on?

11. What teams played in the Bacardi Bowl?

12. When was the forward pass legalized?

13. Which two colleges have met the greatest number of times?

14. What college player holds the record for the longest punt?

15. Who is the only player to win the Heisman Trophy twice?

16. What teams were involved in the famous 1940 "Fifth-down" game?

17. Where was Knute Rockne, football's winningest coach, born?

18. What team once played five games in six days?

19. Who is known as the "Father of American Football"?

20. Who ran the wrong way in the 1929 Rose Bowl game?

21. Which teams played in the first televised football game?

22. What team was characterized by "Three yards and a cloud of dust"?

23. When was the two-point conversion rule put into effect?

24. What former All-America honoree is now a U.S. Supreme Court justice?

25. When were the goal posts moved back 10 yards from the goal line?

26. What does KF-79 refer to?

27. What team was known as the "Prayin' Colonels"?

28. Who was the "Wheaton Iceman"?

29. What player made the number 98 famous?

30. What team featured a unit called the "Chinese Bandits"?

31. What universities were once known as (a) Henry Kendall, and (b) Add Ran College?

32. How many four-year colleges had varsity football programs in 1979: (a) 512 (b) 751 (c) 643?

33. What schools play for the Golden Egg Trophy?

34. What do O.J. Simpson's initials stand for?

35. What is the most popular nickname of college football teams?

36. Who was the last player to gain consensus All-America honors at two colleges?

37. What team hasn't had a losing season since 1938?

38. When was the first Homecoming game held?

39. What player gained All-America honors at two positions the same season?

40. What team gained tremendous recognition with the description "undefeated, untied, unscored on, and uninvited"?

41. What team was known as "The Vow Boys"?

42. What was the attendance at the first Army–Navy game in 1890?

43. What coach popularized the flea-flicker play?

44. What two teams played three straight scoreless ties against each other in 1935, 1936, and 1937?

45. What American president threatened to ban football if its brutality was not eliminated?

46. Who was "the lonely end"?

47. What team had twenty-two Phi Beta Kappas on it?

48. Alabama passed Stanford dizzy in the 1935 Rose Bowl game. Don Hutson was the big receiver; who was the passer?

49. In what game did two teams punt a total of sixty-three times?

50. Who were the "Iron Men"?

ANSWERS

1. *Harry Stuhldreher, quarterback; Jim Crowley, left halfback; Don Miller, right halfback; Elmer Layden, fullback.*

2. *Amos Alonzo Stagg won 244 games as coach at Chicago.*

3. *The 1942 Rose Bowl game, Duke vs. Oregon State, was played at Durham, North Carolina, because of wartime travel limitations.*

4. *Georgia Tech defeated Cumberland, 220-0 in 1916.*

5. *Hardin-Simmons played in the Grape, Shrine, and Camelia Bowls in 1948.*

6. *Washington was undefeated in sixty-three games, 1907-17.*

7. *Bennie Oosterbaan won with Michigan in 1948, his first year.*

8. *Yale's 701 victories through the 1979 season is a record.*

9. *Rutgers and Princeton played the first intercollegiate game on November 6, 1869.*

10. *Tennessee was undefeated, untied, and unscored upon in 1939.*

11. *Auburn and Villanova played in the Bacardi Bowl in Havana on January 1, 1937.*

12. *The forward pass was legalized in 1906.*

13. *Lafayette and Lehigh, both in Pennsylvania, played 115 times through 1979.*

14. *Pat Brady, of Nevada-Reno, booted a 99-yard punt against Loyola of California, 1950.*

15. *Archie Griffin, of Ohio State, won the Heisman Trophy in 1974 and 1975.*

16. *Dartmouth and Cornell were in the 1940 Fifth-Down game. Dartmouth was declared the winner, 3-0.*

17. *Knute Rockne was born in Voss, Norway.*

18. *Sewanee played five games in six days, in 1899. Sewanee is now called the University of the South.*

19. *Walter Camp is known as "The Father of American Football".*

20. *Roy Riegels ran the wrong way in the 1929 Rose Bowl game. His California team lost to Georgia Tech, 8–7.*

21. *Fordham and Waynesburg played in the first televised game, 1939.*

22. *Ohio State was described as "Three yards and a cloud of dust".*

23. *The two-point conversion rule went into effect in 1958.*

24. *Whizzer White, Colorado All-America in 1937, is now Mr. Justice Byron White.*

25. *The goal posts were moved back 10 yards from the goal line in 1927.*

26. *KF-79 was the spinner play on which Al Barabas of Columbia scored against heavily favored Stanford in the 1934 Rose Bowl to win 7–0.*

27. *The team of Centre College, in Kentucky, was known as the "Prayin' Colonels".*

28. *Red Grange was the Wheaton Iceman. He had a job delivering ice during his summer vacation. He needed the money, as he did not have a scholarship at the University of Illinois.*

29. *Tom Harmon, later a famous announcer, wore No. 98 at Michigan.*

30. *Louisiana State's defensive unit in 1958 under Paul Dietzel was known as "The Chinese Bandits".*

31. *The University of Tulsa was Henry Kendall, and Add Ran College became Texas Christian.*

32. *Six hundred and forty-three four-year colleges had varsity football in 1979.*

33. *Mississippi and Mississippi State play for the Golden Egg Trophy.*

34. *O.J. Simpson's full name is Orenthal James Simpson.*

35. *Twenty-eight NCAA teams have "Tigers" as a nickname; "Bulldogs" is second with eighteen.*

36. *Alex Agase, Purdue, 1943, and Illinois, 1946, was the last man to make consensus All-America at two colleges.*

37. *Penn State has not had a losing season since 1938.*

38. *The first Homecoming game was in 1910, with Illinois hosting Chicago.*

39. *Bronko Nagurski made All-America at both tackle and fullback playing for Minnesota in 1929.*

40. *Colgate was the undefeated, untied, unscored-on team that was uninvited to the Rose Bowl in 1932.*

41. *Stanford's 1934–35 teams were known as the "Vow Boys." They had taken a vow never to be beaten by Southern California—and they weren't.*

42. *The first Army–Navy game in 1890 drew 300 spectators.*

43. *Bob Zuppke of Illinois popularized the flea-flicker play.*

44. *Fordham and Pittsburgh played three successive scoreless ties in 1935, 1936, and 1937.*

45. *President Theodore Roosevelt, in 1905, threatened to ban football for its brutality after a number of fatal accidents.*

46. *Bill Carpenter of Army, in 1958, was "the lonely end" who lined up at a distance from the rest of his team and did not return to the huddle.*

47. *Dartmouth's 1925 team had twenty-two Phi Beta Kappas on it.*

48. *Dixie Howell did the passing for Alabama in the 1935 Rose Bowl game against Stanford.*

49. *In 1946 East Texas State and Sam Houston punted a total of sixty-three times in their game.*

50. *"The Iron Men" were Brown's 1926 unbeaten team.*

They're *Still* Speaking Our Language

If you've made it through the earlier tangle of football-talk with its obscure speech patterns and lingual shorthand, here's another delivery of the same material. Wade through this and you've won an up-front spot in the next Thursday night's game-plan meeting.

1. Cadence
2. Containment
3. Crossblock
4. Cutback
5. Cut block
6. Flare action
7. Flood patterns
8. I-formation
9. Keys, or "to key"
10. Line calls
11. Nose guard
12. Option
13. Pinch
14. Play action
15. Rollout
16. Sack
17. Slot formation
18. Strong
19. Weak
20. Split the seams

21. Stats
22. Statue of Liberty
23. Suicide squad
24. Taxi squad
25. Turk walks
26. Two-minute series
27. Waffled
28. Wild card
29. Wrinkle

ANSWERS

1. *Cadence: The rhythm with which the quarterback calls plays at the line of scrimmage. A staggered cadence is often used to draw the defense offside.*

2. *Containment: This is a primary assignment for cornerbacks and safeties on running plays. The ball carrier is funneled toward the middle of the field and into the pursuit of linebackers.*

3. *Crossblock: A type of block in which the tackle and guard exchange blocking assignments.*

4. *Cutback: The correct tactic for turning running plays inside. A defender (usually a linebacker or a defensive back) maintains position on the runner and forces him outside.*

5. *Cut Block: Type of blocking technique in which the offensive linemen drive at the defenders' legs. Particularly useful in handling quick pass rushers.*

6. *Flare action: A responsibility of running backs is to check on whether a linebacker is blitzing. If not, then the runner is expected to become part of the pass pattern. If the linebacker does blitz, the running back is supposed to stay in the backfield and protect the quarterback by "picking up" the blitz.*

7. *Flood patterns: A predesigned pass pattern in which more than one receiver is expected to penetrate a specific zone or area, thereby forcing changes in primary defensive coverages.*

8. *I-formation: Where the running backs are aligned in a single file behind the quarterback.*

9. *Keys, or "to key": Predisposed moves in various formations that indicate what kind of play is going to develop, either run or pass. Defenders are schooled in what to expect; then they "key" on what their positional opponents will do in particular situations.*

10. *Line calls: Signals called by the offensive center to instruct the rest of his linemates in using either even or odd blocking.*

11. *Nose guard: The lone remaining defensive tackle in the* *three-man defensive line, whose primary assignment is to line up directly opposite the center.*

12. *Option: The option usually starts out as a run but can be switched to a pass, depending on the defense's reaction. If the defensive backs and linebackers overreact to the look of the running play, either the quarterback or the runner has the "option" of throwing the ball to what they hope will be receivers who are not covered.*

13. *Pinch: A "stunt" in which two or more defensive linemen attack the gap prior to the snap of the ball and seek to overpower a single blocker.*

14. *Play action: The quarterback fakes a handoff to one or both backs, hoping to make the linebackers commit themselves to either pass or run coverage. Then the passer drops back and throws.*

15. *Rollout: A movement favored by quarterbacks seeking to offset a strong and quick pass rush. The passer rolls out behind the flow of the offensive blockers and usually throws the ball on the run.*

16. *Sack: Defenders getting to the quarterback before he is able to get rid of the ball. It's a prize rated as highly by linemen and linebackers as an interception by a defending back.*

17. *Slot formation: Two receivers line up on the same side of the field, with the split end spread wide and the flanker lined up inside, and one of them a yard back of the line of scrimmage.*

18. *Strong: Describing the side of the formation on offense featuring two receivers, usually a wide receiver and a tight end.*

19. *Weak: The side of the formation away from the tight end.*

20. *Split the seams: Zone defenses provide for a corner back or safety to be responsible for a definite area. The point where his responsibility ends and his teammate's begins is known as "the seam." The good quarterback targets his passes for this location; the excellent quarterback hits his mark there, in which case he is described as "having split the seams."*

21. *Stats: An abbreviation for "statistics," which have come to be a vital part of the game's strategy. Coaches study stats the way horseplayers study charts, and stats also play a large role in* *evaluating personnel in possible trades. Up to the 1930s they were given scant consideration; in fact the NFL was in business for twelve years before someone thought enough of statistics to pay someone to keep them. And before that time college stats weren't much either, compared to today when they're fed into computers just like income tax returns and census reports.*

22. *Statue of Liberty: An old gimmick, traced to a college beginning, where the quarterback stands there, arm upraised as though to pass, and a runner comes around behind him and snatches the ball from his grasp. Hoary deception but it works a lot.*

23. *Suicide squad: Another name for the special teams. It might not be guaranteed suicide when two heavily encased runners, moving approximately 13 miles an hour, smash headlong into each other, but it certainly is interesting.*

24. *Taxi squad: Same as "cab" squad.*

25. *Turk walks: A pro expression exclusively. It means that you're being cut from the squad. The announcement comes from an emissary, usually an assistant equipment manager who says, "Coach wants to see you in his office. Bring your playbook." Gradually this emissary, for reasons unknown, has come to be known as the Turk. One pro club drove the cut-unfortunates nuts by having a "Turk" who stammered. His listeners would die 1,000 deaths while he struggled to get his message out. Why Turk and not say Bulgar? Or Peruvian? No one will ever know.*

26. *Two-minute series: When a game turns into a "cliff-hanger" (see "cliff-hanger"), the two-minute series comes into action. Teams train for what to do if they're behind with two minutes left. All sorts of contingencies are planned for, including running off successive plays without wasting a half minute in a huddle. John Unitas, who led the Baltimore Colts to several championships, was the acknowledged master of the two-minute series. In fact, he was said to have a fondness for being behind with two minutes to play.*

27. *Waffled: Term for someone being flattened, decked, stretched out, etc. "Flat as a waffle," as it were.*

28. *Wild card: A development in the pros whereby a team out of the contention after the regular season of play can have a second chance in the play-offs. It is based on a superior record over that of* *other second-place teams in other divisions. Originally there was one wild card, but TV demands for extra post-season games have made the wild-card thing a little silly. We may all live to see the time there'll be more teams remaining than have been eliminated following regular season play.*

29. *Wrinkle: A formation usually depending on a surprise element put into an otherwise orthodox game.*

More
Nicknames

Here we go with a second batch of nicknames that made the headlines in the days when their owners were making football history. As Bill Shakespeare (the bard, not the Notre Dame ball player of the thirties) said: "A rose by any name would smell as sweet." Try your sense of smell on these:

1. Doc Blanchard
2. Albie Booth
3. Bad News Cafego
4. Red Cagle
5. Ziggie Czarobski
6. Red Flaherty
7. Biggie Goldberg
8. Buckets Goldenberg
9. Bones Hamilton
10. Brud Holland
11. Dixie Howell
12. Jabo Jablonsky
13. Choo-choo Justice
14. Pug Lund
15. Bo McMillin
16. Chub Peabody
17. Buster Ramsey
18. Horse Reynolds
19. Monk Simons
20. Catfish Smith
21. Eric the Red

22. Cotton Warburton
23. Tarzan White
24. The Team Called "Desire"
25. The Fearsome Foursome
26. The Baby Bulls

ANSWERS

1. *Felix Blanchard (also known as "Mr. Inside" at West Point)*
2. *Albert Booth*
3. *George Cafego*
4. *Christian Cagle*
5. *Zygmont Czarobski*
6. *Ray Flaherty*
7. *Marshall Goldberg*
8. *Charles Goldenberg*
9. *Robert Hamilton*
10. *Jerome Holland*
11. *Millard Howell*
12. *Harvey Jablonsky*
13. *Charles Justice*
14. *Francis Lund*
15. *Alvin McMillin*
16. *Endicott Peabody*
17. *Garrard Ramsey*
18. *Robert Reynolds*
19. *Claude Simons*
20. *Vernon Smith*
21. *Eric Tipton*
22. *Irvine Warburton*
23. *Arthur White*
24. *Navy's 1955 team*
25. *The Los Angeles Rams' defensive line*
26. *The New York Giants' running backs*

And now the first half is over,
so let's go to the . . .

Half-Time Show

YOU FORGOT THE ROLLS

The late Herman Hickman was an All-America lineman at Tennessee a half-century ago, later a pro star with the Brooklyn Dodgers, and an Ivy League head coach at Yale. In his last capacity he was called upon to make recruiting trips, and on them he gave hotel dining rooms a pretty good workout. Herman was a 300-pounder and required more sustenance than the average person.

Herman found himself wide awake at seven o'clock one morning, alone in a hotel room, hungry enough to gnaw on the night table. He reached for the phone and asked for room service. His hillbilly accents came rolling across the wire to the woman taking his order.

"Ah feel a lil' hongry this mawnin'," said Herman, "think Ah'll have me a good breakfast. "Les' start with a double orange juice, a big bowl of oatmeal, two fried eggs 'n a rasher of bacon. Y'got any grits? Mebbe there are some of them banquet rolls left over from last night, and send a big pot of coffee. And, oh yes, mebbe a Danish or two."

The woman on the other end, writing feverishly, thanked him and went to hang up. But Hickman had been having second thoughts. "Wait a minute," he said. "I got a friend here who's a little hongry, too. Send him the same."

THE GOOD OLD DAYS

In the half-forgotten pioneer days of the NFL, the Orange (N.J.) Athletic Club made a brief appearance in the competitive lists. It was followed the next year by a club called the Newark (N.J.) Tornadoes. Same club—at least same promoter.

Fellow's name was Piggy (real first name unknown) Simandl, and he was a sports promoter of sorts around Newark. It was no trouble then getting into the NFL. A $500-franchise would do it. Frequently the franchise payment still wasn't made when the season ended.

Wellington Mara recalls going over to Newark with the New York Giants to play the Orange A.C. It was a regularly scheduled league game. "When we got there," recalled Mara, "they only had ten men. So we lent them a man. I don't remember whether it was a back or a lineman. He probably played both positions."

Simandl chronically ran a trifle short and the players frequently failed to collect their fifty or seventy-five dollars a game. After he ran up a tab of a few weeks on one performer, the player said he'd quit if he didn't get his money. Simandl told him there were a lot of players around. So the man disappeared.

Shortly thereafter Simandl got a wire from the Providence Steam Roller, another pioneer team in Rhode Island, offering a $5,000-guarantee for a postseason game. The telegram suggested that Simandl meet the Providence representative in a New York hotel lobby the next day at noon. Piggy put on his best suit and hustled over to New York. Promptly at noon a stranger came up and asked whether he was Piggy Simandl? Piggy beamed assent, whereupon the stranger dropped a summons on him. The unpaid player had gotten himself a lawyer in an effort to collect his back salary and had figured out a sure way to serve Piggy with the summons.

HAIL TO THEE, OH PLAINFIELD TEACHERS

Finest football hoax in history involved a mythical college football team that sprang, full-blown, from the forehead of a fun-
loving New York stockbroker forty years ago. Plainfield
Teachers' story is still a fresh one, with its star Chinese
halfback, and its tricky formation, and its being caught red-
headed with two games of a nonexistent schedule remaining. It
has been retold a dozen times in print. It was even done for TV.

Morris Newberger was a University of Pennsylvania alum-
nus who used to tell his friends he didn't believe some of those
schools existed when he rummaged through the Sunday morning football scores checking on his alma mater. To prove it he
set up a fake school, gave it a football team, a coach, publicity
man, and a destiny (the Blackboard Bowl) and proceeded to
obtain all kinds of publicity for it.

Newberger's attack was frontal. He simply made a half
dozen nickel phone calls to the biggest papers in New York on
a Saturday afternoon, an hour or two after what would normal-
ly have been the end of a game, and said he wanted to report a
college football score. He spoke in well-modulated tones, as
though he was handling some customer placing an order for
20,000 shares of stock.

Everyone took the bait. There was "Plainfield Teachers" the
following morning, nestled between his alma mater, Pennsylvania, and Princeton. His first victory. "Winona," a name
that sounds as honest as a government bond, was the loser.

There was another victory the following Saturday, this one
over "Randolph Tech". He permitted Randolph to get one
touchdown to Plainfield's five. No sense being greedy.

During the week Newberger decided the team needed a lit-
tle additional publicity, so he had his phantom publicity man,
Jerry Croyden, send out a press release praising the abilities of
Plainfield's dynamic halfback, John Chung, a Chinese ex-
change student. Chung, as pointed out by Newberger-
Croyden, had a stout leg up on his rivals. Between halves they

would rush him a bowl of rice, which he would gulp down for renewed vigor.

"Scott" hit the deck, followed by "St. Joseph's" (the current list of St. Josephses with varsity football teams includes schools in Philadelphia and Indiana, so one more wouldn't make too much difference) and there was a big one coming up with "Appalachian Teachers", in which Chung was supposed to get hurt but come off the bench and help win 20-2. Then there'd be the big one over "Harmony Teachers" that would put Plainfield Teachers into the "Blackboard Bowl" against a rival to be named.

Newberger couldn't keep from sharing the fun with his friends in Wall Street, however, and *Time* Magazine got wind of it. They ran an expose, stopping Plainfield Teachers' unbeaten and untied streak and putting its mythical press agent, Jerry Croyden and its even more mythical coach, Harry (Hurry-Up) Hoblitzel, into the ranks of the unemployed.

Newberger went down with Plainfield's puce and ecru colors nailed to the mast—pardon, the goal posts. He sent a release to the papers announcing that Chung and eleven other varsity men had flunked midterm exams and were no longer eligible. The school therefore was dissolving the team and forfeiting the remainder of the schedule.

So Plainfield Teachers, with its radical "W" formation (the ends lined up *looking* at the quarterback, to get a better idea of what was going on), was no more. It disappeared, although some thoughtful historian remembered to salvage the school's alma mater which, to the tune of Cornell University's "Far Above Cayuga's Waters," went something like this:

> *Far above New Jersey's swamplands*
> *Plainfield Teachers' spires*
> *Mark a phantom, phoney college*
> *That got on the wires.*
> *Perfect record made on paper,*
> *Imaginary team*
> *Hail to thee, our ghostly college*
> *Product of a dream!*

TOO DUMB TO REMEMBER THE PLAYS . . .

Ever hear of a pro quarterback named Vic Eaton? If you haven't, don't be embarrassed. He was only a third-stringer and he stuck around just one year with a club that was 4–and–8 for the season. He threw the ball only twice and did some punting. He also changed the course of pro football history.

Vic Eaton, out of Missouri, was the rookie Pittsburgh kept when they cut John Unitas in 1955. The Steelers had Jim Finks, who was a first-class quarterback, as their starter, plus a No.-1 draft pick, Ted Marichibroda, returning from the service. Johnny Unitas and Vic Eaton were draft picks so far down the list that no one, including Pittsburgh, figured any immediate help to be forthcoming from either of these sources.

Unitas thought he had the edge on staying. He was a local boy, and owner Art Rooney's son Dan had played against him in a Pittsburgh high school championship.

But the football bounces peculiarly, on and off the field. There were two developments during the exhibition season that set back the running schedule for Pittsburgh's winning a championship a couple of decades.

First there was the clash between Finks and the coach, Walt Kiesling. Finks made light of something Kiesling said during practice and Kiesling fired him on the spot. Finks was going, too, except that they somehow found Art Rooney via a transcontinental phone call and Rooney talked his No.-1 quarterback into staying. Had he gone, it would have meant keeping both rookies to back up Marichibroda (who later was to become a major-league coach himself).

The other development was that Eaton got into an exhibition game against the powerful L.A. Rams and demonstrated an ability to move the Steelers. And he could punt, too—not well enough to be up there with the league leaders at the end of the campaign but better than anyone else on the club.

So Unitas was given his walking papers and when Rooney asked his coach for an explanation, Kiesling said, "He can't remember the plays, he's too dumb to do it." You have to have some excuse for cutting a kid you haven't seen. Unitas had never had a minute of playing time with the Steelers.

The rest is fairly familiar football history—how Unitas played semi-pro that season for six dollars a game with a sandlot team called the Bloomfield Rams; how Don Kellett, general manager of the Baltimore Colts, combing some old waiver lists, discovered Unitas's name after the season. Kellert put in a claim for him in January after contacting him by phone, a call estimated as costing eighty cents, making it the biggest bargain in the history of the telephone company. Unitas immediately embarked upon a long, distinguished career that led to Hall of Fame honors and his selection as the all-time quarterback in the history of the N.F.L.

But that isn't the complete story. Years later Eaton, in the jewelry business in the midwest (his company does most of the Super Bowl rings), recalled that he was almost as puzzled about being kept by the Steelers as Unitas was over being cut.

"I had a commitment to the Air Force after ROTC work at school. It was for four years and I told the Steelers about it, that I'd be there only for a year. I guess they thought I was fooling or something."

Eaton did meet his commitment to Uncle Sam and went the four-year distance. When he came out he felt that he didn't have the time to try to make it as a pro football player, and he entered business. And every Monday morning in the fall he'd turn to the sports pages and read about Johnny Unitas and the Baltimore Colts, then riding high as world champions.

THAT MAN OVER THERE SAID SO . . .

Ernie Stautner and Rosey Brown are co-occupants of the Hall
of Fame at Canton. They played on rival teams, Stautner with
Pittsburgh and Rosey with the New York Giants. Stautner was a
defensive tackle while Brown was an offensive tackle. That
meant that twice a year they'd bump heads and other portions.
Their clashes would sometimes reach awesome proportions
because these were stand-out strong men in a business where
strength is pretty much a commonplace.

Age caught up with Stautner first and he retired to become
an assistant with the Steelers' coaching staff. Brown stayed a
couple of additional seasons and found himself opposing a
tough young kid named Ben McGee, who had come to the
Pittsburgh team from Jackson State. No Hall of Famer but plenty tough. Also he was holding Brown just a bit more than most,
but Rosey shrugged it off as an example of the overzealousness
of youth.

The second time they played that season, however, Brown
found himself becoming irritated. The kid was holding more.
A lot more. "Don't do that," he snapped, "you're holding. It
ain't allowed."

The kid mumbled something about its "being all right."

On the very next play there were those clutching fingers
again. Now Rosey was good and sore, sore at both the kid and
at the officials for not picking it up. "Don't do that again, kid,"
he warned, "or you'll be goddam sorry."

"It's all right," said McGee. Rosey couldn't believe he had
heard correctly.

"Whaddya mean it's 'all right?'"

"They told me it was all right to hold," said the youngster.

"Who told you?" demanded Brown.

"Mr. Stautner," said the young man.

DON'T SPEND IT ALL IN ONE PLACE

The late Jimmy Conzelman, another pro Hall of Famer, coached off and on in the NFL for twenty years but didn't come up with a championship until late, when his '47 Chicago Cards beat Philadelphia. First, the Cards had to get past their intra-city rivals, the big, bad Chicago Bears, and it came down to a final game with them for Western Conference title.

It was played at Wrigley Field, and Conzelman brought his small son along as a good luck charm—and also because the kid wanted to see the game. He had him on the sideline with him during the game, a dramatic one that seesawed all over the place. Late in the third quarter, with his gaze glued to the action on the field, Conzelman suddenly felt a tug on his pants leg. He looked down for a split second. It was the kid.

"Whaddya want?"

"I wanna' quarter for a hot dog," said the kid.

Conzelman felt around in his pocket and came up with a fifty-cent piece.

He handed it to his son without looking. "Here," he said, "bring change."

AND NO ONE ELSE?

Y.A. Tittle, Hall of Fame quarterback, labored for the San Francisco 49ers for more than a decade without getting even a whiff of any postseason play-off money. At the end he failed to fit in with a new shotgun "spread" offense. Then came a touch of the magic wand when Wellington Mara, the New York Giants talent director, caught the 49ers off balance and swung a deal for Tittle, trading a journeyman defensive lineman named Lou Cordileone for Y.A. It was to result in the Giants making the play-offs three straight years in the early sixties.

The news was a little slow getting to the Giants training camp. Cordileone was welcoming and congratulating Tittle along with the other Giants when someone told him he was the man who had been traded to get Tittle.

"Me?" said Cordileone a little incredulously, "and who else?"

TAKE CARE OF UNCLE BURRIS

The pro record book shows five quarterbacks credited with seven TDs in a game. Included in this group was the eggshell-bald Y.A. Tittle, who did it late in his career. He threw seven for the New York Giants in 1962 against the Washington Redskins and it brought him immediate national notice, something that was lacking in the days when he played for the 49ers.

The following week the Giants were scheduled to play in Dallas and it figured to be a big afternoon for the New York team and Tittle. For one thing, the Dallas of the early sixties was a far cry from the juggernaut that shows up in postseason play today. For another, Y.A. was from Marshall, Texas, and the word was that half the town, most of whom were related, planned to show up.

Don Smith, the Giants press agent, scouted up fifty tickets for Tittle's kith and kin. When he handed them to Y.A., Tittle said, "Hope you didn't forget Uncle Burris," referring to the patriarch of the clan. "Gotta take care of Uncle Burris."

Because of taking care of Uncle B. and the rest, Tittle's routine was all screwed up. No quiet meal the night before the game, no watching "Gunsmoke" with teammate Del Shofner, no meeting the following morning with Coach Allie Sherman on last-minute strategy. Just a lot of hooting and hollering with relatives who were finding it difficult to believe that Y.A. had become a national figure and that all them fellas with the pencils were asking him questions, and didn't he answer that one before?

Tittle got into the game, his head whirling a bit. He tried a screen pass to Joe Morrison and here came big Bob Lilly to pick it off. Tittle was the last man to have a shot at Lilly as he sped goalward, and it was, of course, no match.

As Tittle lay flattened on the Cotton Bowl's grass, he raised himself on one elbow, clenched the fist of his other hand and pounded the turf.

"Goddam you, Uncle Burris," he shouted.

LOMBARDI'S WAY

Jim Ringo was an All-League center whose career began in 1953 with the Green Bay Packers and ended in 1967. During that time, the Packers won all kinds of championships, including the first two Super Bowls, and the very word "Packer" became synonymous with formidable strength.

Ringo had a piece of that action through 1963, and finished the last segment of his pro experience elsewhere. And thereby dangles a story of Vince Lombardi's unconcealed scorn for player agents, whom he placed in the same category as the people coming around to collect the rent when he was a kid growing up in Brooklyn.

The Packers won in 1961 and 1962, and finished behind the surprising Bears in '63. The margin wasn't much. The Bears were 11-1-2, and the Packers were 11-2-1. Lombardi never liked to lose, and he was sitting in his sumptuous office in the sumptuous stadium that the grateful Green Bay people had built for him wondering whether it was possible that HE hadn't made a mistake somewhere along the line.

A caller was announced. It was a gracious young man who introduced himself, handing Lombardi his card and announcing he was Jim Ringo's agent. Lombardi gave the card his best stare, meanwhile pulling on his lower lip, the one that had required thirteen stitches after the last of three successive Fordham–Pittsburgh scoreless ties back in the thirties. No masks in those days.

Finally he looked up. "Who did you say you represent?" he asked. The young man was slightly startled. "Jim Ringo," he said.

"Just a minute," said Lombardi, and he got up and went outside.

He tapped his secretary on the shoulder and said, "Get me Vince McNally in Philadelphia," he said. McNally was the general manager of the Philadelphia Eagles in the other NFL division. Lombardi waited a short time and then returned to his office.

He had barely gotten back into his chair when McNally was on the phone.

"Will you excuse me, please?" Lombardi said to the visitor, "I have an important matter to discuss with this caller. I won't be too long. You can wait outside."

Ten minutes later Lombardi buzzed and asked that the young man be sent in. "Now," Lombardi said, "what was it you wanted?"

The young fellow stared at Lombardi's craggy face. Obviously he was dealing with a lunatic, although one who could win in the National Football League. But the stakes were high, so he went through his routine again, explaining he was representing Jim Ringo, Lombardi's starting center, and he'd like to discuss Ringo's contract for 1964.

Lombardi looked at him as though he had flunked an early-morning quiz. "There must be some mistake, young man," he said, "Jim Ringo doesn't play for the Packers. He's a member of the Philadelphia Eagles. You'd better get in touch with them."

In the interlude that the agent had been cooling his heels in the anteroom, Lombardi had traded his center for a couple of draft choices.

IT'S ALREADY BEEN MAILED

Ever get that sinking feeling that something was amiss 30 seconds after you dropped that letter in the mailbox? Football Hall of Famer Mel Hein, an All-America at Washington State, escaped that sensation when he sent back his first signed pro football contract, but he got it full blast the next day when he got a better offer from another club.

He had signed with the Providence Steam Roller back East at a modest salary and here was a better deal from a much better club, the New York Giants. What to do?

"I was friendly with the postmaster in Pullman, Washington, and he said if I would pay for the cost of the wire he'd get a message to the postmaster in Providence to short-circuit the letter and get it back to me. The telegram was only a couple of cents in those days. In a few days I had the contract back, unopened. I guess there was a lot less red tape then."

Especially if you were an All-America and a Rose Bowl hero.

Mel later went on to play for fifteen years with the Giants, made All-League many times, and was in the original group inducted into pro Hall of Fame in 1963.

I CAN'T GAIN ON HIM, COACH

George Halas, founder and only owner ever of the Chicago Bears, coached his club for forty years in four ten-year segments, which is a record that will never be eclipsed. How did he know when to pack it in finally and unequivocably?

"It was easy," recalled Halas. "We got socked with a 15-yard penalty and I was standing right there when the official bent down to pick up the ball to walk off the yards. He started walking and I started running along the sideline, still arguing about the call. I knew it was the end when he was just walking and I couldn't keep up with him."

THEM VIRUSES WILL GETCHA EVERY TIME

During Weeb Ewbank's tenure as head coach of the New York Jets, he had a massive defensive lineman who was bigger than he was bright. He was also a trifle careless in his social dealings. He came up with the same venereal disease twice in a season, which is NOT a record among professional athletes.

To maintain the proper image among their followers, the Jets gave out the word that the big fellow had been the victim of a "virus". And when he was sidelined again, well, the "virus" had reappeared. It was apparently a big season for virulent viruses. The lineman played a total of two games.

Naturally, that winter he wanted a raise.

"A raise?" shrieked Ewbank, who was brought up on the midwest ethic of a day's pay for a day's work. "You only played in two goddam games the whole year."

"Well, coach," said the big guy, "you know I had them viruses."

THIRD QUARTER

More
"Who Said"?

1. "A tie is like kissing your sister"?

2. "It's kinda hard to rally 'round a math class"?

3. "Behind every fired head football coach stands a college president"?

4. "The idea is to win just enough to keep the alumni sullen instead of mutinous"?

5. "If you really want to advise me, do it on Saturday afternoon between 1 and 4. And you got 25 seconds between plays. Not on Monday. I know the right thing to do on Monday"?

6. "Gentlemen, you are about to play Harvard. Never again in your lives will you do anything so important"?

7. "He must have played too many games without his helmet"?

8. "You can't play two kinds of football at once, good and dirty"?

9. "If you aren't fired with enthusiasm you'll be fired with enthusiasm"?

10. "Two out of three ain't bad"?

11. "During the week I practice law; on Sunday I AM the law"?

12. "I don't know what to say; I'm waiting for the bench to send in a statement"?

[84]

13. "It would have been 73–7"?

14. "He tosses nickels around like manhole covers"?

15. "The most enjoyable part of pro football is being introduced and running onto the field. Everything after that is downhill"?

16. "I have never knowingly bit another football player. One thing I believe in is good hygiene"?

17. "Never insult the intelligence of your viewer. If you have nothing to say, shut up"?

ANSWERS

1. *Duffy Daugherty, of Michigan State.*

2. *Bear Bryant, of Alabama.*

3. *John McKay, of Southern California.*

4. *The late Herman Hickman, coaching at Yale.*

5. *Alex Agase, Purdue.*

6. *Tad Jones, at Yale.*

7. *Lyndon Johnson, discussing Gerald Ford, who had been an all-Big Ten center.*

8. *Glenn S. (Pop) Warner, of Stanford.*

9. *Vince Lombardi, at Green Bay.*

10. *Tex Schramm, boss of Dallas, following a verbal attack by Cowboy running back Duane Thomas, in which he called Schramm "a liar, a thief and a crook".*

11. *Tommy Bell, the No.-1 referee in pro football for more than a decade. He worked more Super Bowl games at his position than any other official.*

12. *Roger Staubach, Dallas Cowboys quarterback, receiving one of his many trophies. Staubach was taking a sly shot at Tom Landry's calling the plays for him to execute from the sideline.*

13. *Sammy Baugh's wry comment when he was asked what would have happened in the 1941 NFL championship game, won by the Chicago Bears 73–0, if one of the Redskin receivers hadn't dropped his pass in the end zone?*

14. *Tight end Mike Ditka's description of Chicago owner George Halas's attitude toward a buck. In fairness to Halas, no one ever came ringing his door bell in the pioneer days when George had to play with one eye on the opposing quarterback, the other eye on the gent who was handling the box office take for him.*

15. *Doug Swift, a Miami Dolphins linebacker.*

16. *Conrad Dobler, St. Louis Cardinals lineman who came equipped with a large ego, large muscles, and large teeth.*

17. *Advice offered other TV announcers by Paul Christman, who made the move from quarterbacking the Chicago Cardinals to handling the early AFL network broadcasts. The commentator believed that people who listened did so for information, not entertainment.*

Christman had been an All-America at the University of Missouri and was a successful contractor in the off-season.

Something to Take Home

The oldest football trophy is the Little Brown Jug, which actually *is* a five-gallon earthenware jug colored brown. It is a Big Ten fixture and it goes back to the time when a visiting trainer thought he'd better bring along some water, just in case. There was some question of ownership, and the team that originally brought it found that possession had passed to the home team with the·suggestion, "If you want your jug back come back next year and beat us."

There are all kinds of football trophies, some elaborate affairs, some dime-store productions, and some objets d'art fished out of a trash can en route to the game. No matter what the material value, they're competed for as enthusiastically as though they were the keys to Fort Knox.

Here are some of them. If you can identify more than a half dozen, you've really been around—or you've read a lot of college football brochures.

1. Alumni Governor's Cup
2. Axe Trophy
3. Broomhead Trophy
4. Centennial Trophy
5. Chief Caddo Trophy
6. Golden Egg Trophy
7. Heisman Trophy
8. Little Brown Jug

9. Little Brown Stein
10. Maxwell Trophy
11. Megaphone Trophy
12. Mission Bell Trophy
13. Old Brass Spittoon
14. Old Ironsides
15. Old Wagon Wheel
16. Outland Trophy
17. Peace Pipe
18. Rag Trophy
19. Sabine Shoe Trophy
20. The Shillelagh
21. Silver Shako

ANSWERS

1. *Alumni Governor's Cup: Dartmouth vs. Princeton. The late Nelson Rockefeller, a former Dartmouth soccer player, picked up the tab on this one.*

2. *Axe Trophy: California vs. Stanford*

3. *Broomhead Trophy: Brown vs. Rhode Island (for the championship of the smallest state in the Union)*

4. *Centennial Trophy: Princeton-Rutgers, honoring the oldest of football rivalries*

5. *Chief Caddo Trophy: Stephen Austin vs. Northwest Louisiana*

6. *Golden Egg Trophy: Mississippi vs. Mississippi State*

7. *Heisman Trophy: Top individual trophy in the nation*

8. *Little Brown Jug: Michigan vs. Minnesota, going back to the horse-and-wagon days*

9. *Little Brown Stein: Not nearly as old. Prize for the competition between Montana and Idaho*

10. *Maxwell Trophy: Another top-ranking individual trophy*

11. *Megaphone Trophy: Notre Dame vs. Michigan State*

12. *Mission Bell Trophy: Fullerton State vs. Long Beach State, in California*

13. *Old Brass Spittoon: Michigan State-Indiana*

14. *Old Ironsides: Three-way annual trophy involving Penn State, Pittsburgh, and West Virginia University*

15. *Old Wagon Wheel: Brigham Young vs. Utah State, and can't you hear Glenn Ford yelling for the wagons to form a circle?*

16. *Outland Trophy: Individual trophy for the nation's top linemen. They don't get much of a chance at the Heisman.*

17. *Peace Pipe: Oklahoma-Missouri*

18. *Rag Trophy: Banner for Northwest Louisiana-Louisiana Tech*

19. *Sabine Shoe Trophy: Lamar Tech-Southwest Louisiana*

20. *The Shillelagh: Two of these, one for Notre Dame–Southern California, the other for Notre Dame–Purdue*

21. *Silver Shako: Virginia Military Institute vs. The Citadel*

The Biggest Prize

The Heisman Memorial Trophy is the No.-1 football award, college or pro, growing steadily in importance since the first one was given in 1936. Pro football has a half-dozen awards for the top player in the National Football League, ranging from those picked by the wire services to the Seagram's 7 Crowns of Sport winner, which carries with it the not insignificant prize of $10,000.

There are other college awards, but they are invariably diminished by the Heisman, named after an old coach, John W. Heisman. His credits, besides coming up with winners at Georgia Tech, Pennsylvania, W. and J., and Rice, also include the invention of the vocal signal, the direct snap from center, the spinner play, and splitting the game into quarters instead of halves.

The Heisman is awarded at the beginning of December, giving a player's agent plenty of time to scout the pro field on behalf of his client before the pro draft three months later. A financial rule of thumb is that the Heisman award will usually double a player's signing bonus. Some winners haven't fulfilled expectations in the pros (in the past two decades John Huarte, Gary Beban, Steve Spurrier, Steve Owens, Pat Sullivan, and Johnny Rodgers come to mind); but within that span Heisman winners Roger Staubach, Mike Garrett, O.J. Simpson, Archie Griffin, Tony Dorsett, and Earl Campbell have gone on to pro fame.

1. The first Heisman winner was Chicago's Jay Berwanger, a running back. What pro team did he play for?

2. There have been three Ivy League winners. Name them.

3. What Heisman winner wound up an FBI man?

4. Who was the tallest Heisman winner?

5. There have been a total of five Heisman winners from the service academies (Army, Navy, Air Force). Name them.

6. Three schools have had successive winners. Name them.

7. The year Jim Brown was a Syracuse senior and All-America, who won the Heisman?

8. Who was the last nonservice academy Heisman winner who didn't go on to play pro ball?

9. Only two linemen have won the Heisman. Name them.

10. What Heisman winner also played major league baseball?

11. What Heisman winner was killed when his Navy fighter plane crashed in World War II?

12. What Heisman trophy winner became an outstanding sports announcer?

13. What Heisman winner still holds the pro record for most combined yards gained in one game—passing, running, and returns?

14. What school has produced the greatest number of Heisman winners?

15. When Doc Blanchard became the first player to win the Heisman as a junior, who was runner-up?

ANSWERS

1. *Jay Berwanger never played pro. He was drafted by the Philadelphia Eagles and his rights were traded to the Chicago Bears, who didn't sign him even though he was a local boy. Berwanger asked for a two-year contract at $20,000, unheard of figures in '36.*

2. *Ivy League winners have been Larry Kelley, Yale, 1937; Clint Frank, Yale, 1938; and Dick Kazmaier, Princeton, 1951.*

3. *Davey O'Brien, of TCU, 1938 winner, became an FBI man.*

4. *Leon Hart, at an announced 6'5" (he could have been more) was the tallest Heisman winner. He played for the Detroit Lions after leaving Notre Dame.*

5. *The service academy winners were Doc Blanchard, Glenn Davis, and Pete Dawkins, of Army; and Joe Bellino and Roger Staubach, of Navy.*

6. *Schools with successive winners were Yale (Kelley and Frank), Army (Blanchard and Davis), and Ohio State (with Archie Griffin a double winner).*

7. *In Jim Brown's senior year, Paul Hornung, Notre Dame quarterback, was the Heisman winner. Hornung was also the No.-1 pick in the pro draft by Green Bay.*

8. *Pete Dawkins, the 1958 winner, didn't play pro ball. He attended Oxford on a Rhodes scholarship and stayed in the service.*

9. *The two linemen who won were ends Larry Kelley and Leon Hart.*

10. *Vic Janowicz, of Ohio State, the 1950 winner, played pro football (Washington Redskins) and pro baseball (Pittsburgh Pirates). He was a catcher.*

11. *Nile Kinnick, of Iowa, 1939 winner, perished in his Navy plane's crash.*

12. *Tom Harmon, of Michigan, went on to an outstanding career as a sports announcer.*

13. *Billy Cannon, of LSU, won in 1959. In 1961, playing for the*

Houston Oilers in the American Football League against the New York Titans (later the Jets), he totaled 373 yards, rushing, receiving, and returning kicks.

14. *Notre Dame has had the greatest number of Heisman winners, six. Ohio State is second with five.*

15. *When Blanchard won the Heisman, his teammate Glenn Davis was runner-up. The following year Davis won. Many consider that 1945 Army team, muscled-up with war-time personnel, the greatest college team ever assembled. Its coach, Earl Blaik, settled for "This is the greatest team Army ever had."*

The Halls of Academe

The first college football game was played in 1869, and Rutgers beat Princeton. Princeton had challenged Rutgers and the boys from the banks of the Raritan said why not but let's play here at Rutgers.

So the Princetonians took the morning train up to New Brunswick, about a 30-mile run, and they and their backers were given lunch and a tour of the town. Some of the visitors got involved in the billiard parlors, but the rest went out to the field and watched Rutgers win, six goals to four. That was the agreement; first team to get six goals wins. One of Princeton's goals was due to a wrong-way kick by a Rutgers player. Even in that *first* game!

The first organized college cheering was heard at that game. Princeton students had picked it up from soldiers of the 7th New York Regiment, passing through Princeton on their way South during the Civil War.

Two weeks after that first meeting, the Rutgers boys went down to Princeton for a return match. There they had trouble with the ball, which wasn't quite round and couldn't be inflated properly (the inner bladder and canvas cover had just been invented). Princeton's players seemed to have had less trouble than the Rutgers team, because they won 8-0, although history remembers only the first game's score.

The Rutgers-Princeton series was one of the nation's oldest sporting confrontations at the time it was terminated at the start of the 1980s. Rutgers, New Jersey's state university, didn't seem to mind taking an annual licking from Princeton for thirty or forty years, during which Princeton frequently dominated the Ivy League, but when things changed and Rutgers went in

[96]

for big-time football, Princeton figured that tradition was for the history books and ended the meetings. But that was the start.

1. Rutgers was the first suggested home of the College Football Hall of Fame because it was the site of the first game. The idea never got beyond some excavating. Before the Hall eventually landed at King's Island, Ohio, outside Cincinnati, where was it and a lot of its memorabilia located?

2. What are the requirements for a player to be considered for membership?

3. What school has the greatest number of players in the Hall of Fame?

4. Notre Dame's all-time backfield combination, the Four Horsemen, are all in the Hall of Fame. They didn't go in as a unit, however. In what progression were they elected?

5. Dwight Eisenhower, one of the Hall of Fame's Gold Medal winners, is not in the Hall itself as a player. (He played for the U.S. Military Academy.) What is the highest office achieved by a player who *is* in the Hall of Fame?

6. Nordy Hoffman, a Notre Dame guard, went on to a highly specialized U. S. government job. What was it?

7. Jack Cannon, a Notre Dame guard in the late twenties, is in the Hall of Fame. So is another Notre Damer called "The Springfield Rifle". Who was he?

8. What Hall of Famer went to the Rose Bowl with Alabama, liked the climate, stuck around, and became a movie star?

9. The Hall of Fame has given out a dozen or so "Gold Medals" for outstanding citizenship or accomplishment to people connected with football in some capacity. Recipients have included Eisenhower, General MacArthur, Justice Hugo Black, and presidents Ford, Nixon, and

Hoover. Who is the only Gold Medal winner who is also in the Hall of Fame as a player?

10. Amos Alonso Stagg is the only man in the College Hall of Fame to make it both as a player and a coach. He invented a dozen different techniques and coached until he was close to a hundred years old. What record does he hold in the college book?

11. In the College Hall of Fame there is a nook called the "coaches' locker room" where you can sit and hear the famous speech by Rockne in which he tells his team, behind after the first half, how George Gipp told him on his deathbed that when the going got tough he should ask them to "win one for the Gipper." How long did that speech take?

12. Merlin Olsen, All-America at Utah State and all-pro with the Los Angeles Rams, entered the College Hall of Fame in 1980. What was his previous connection with it?

13. A former Navy tackle and Hall of Famer was the supervising officer at the Viet Nam evacuation. Who was he?

14. What Hall of Famer was born in Greece?

15. That was an easy one. Now how about the only Hall of Famer to be born in Australia?

16. The Four Horsemen of Notre Dame will ride forever. Their linemen, the "Seven Mules" don't have nearly that kind of immortality. One of them, however, is in the Hall of Fame. Who is he?

17. One Hall of Famer became one of Hollywood's all-time stunt men and was killed at his work after thirty years. Who was he?

18. Who was the Hall of Famer who played eight years of college ball and didn't raise a peep from any of the eligibility officials?

19. Who was the first person to pick an All-America team? He's in the Hall of Fame, naturally.

20. What Hall of Famer has also been honored by the Academy of Motion Picture Arts and Sciences?

21. It sounds a little corny, but almost fifty years ago a Stanford team coached by Tiny Thornhill took a vow never to lose to Southern California. They became known as the "Vow Boys". How many Rose Bowls did these Vow Boys get to?

22. How many did they win?

23. How many of the "Vow Boys" made the Hall of Fame?

24. The all-time Cotton Bowl backfield of Sammy Baugh, Bobby Layne, John Kimbrough and Dick Maegle are all members of the Hall of Fame. What colleges did they play for?

25. Brick Muller was a California end who never played in a losing game. He is in the Hall of Fame, but what is his special distinction as an All-America?

26. The coaches for both sides in the famous Dartmouth–Cornell "5th Down" game of 1940 are in the Hall of Fame. Who are they?

ANSWERS

1. *Before it reached its present site, on the Interstate between Cincinnati and Columbus, Ohio, the Hall of Fame was in a brownstone on the East Side in New York.*

2. *A player, to be eligible for membership, must be out of school ten years. A coach must be out of coaching for at least three years. Pro experience does not extend the time. In other words, a college star who played pro for ten or eleven years could be eligible immediately.*

3. *Yale and Notre Dame, with twenty-two players each, are tied for the honor of having the greatest number of Hall of Famers. The Yales got an earlier start.*

4. *Elmer Layden was the first of the Four Horsemen selected. He entered in the 1951 charter group. Harry Stuhldreher made it in '58, Jim Crowley in '66, and Don Miller in '70.*

5. *Endicott (Chub) Peabody, a Harvard guard in 1939–41, held the highest elective office. He served as governor of Massachusetts. The highest appointed office achieved was that of U.S. Supreme Court Justice Byron (Whizzer) White, Colorado back.*

6. *Frank (Nordy) Hoffman, former Notre Dame guard, is the sergeant-at-arms of the U.S. Senate. Theoretically, he would be the man to arrest anyone up to and including the president, if necessary.*

7. *Angelo Bertelli was "The Springfield Rifle". He came from Springfield, Massachusetts, where the well-known infantry piece of World Wars I and II was manufactured.*

8. *Johnny Mack Brown played for Alabama in the Rose Bowl, succumbed to the blandishments of sunny southern California, and wound up as an actor in films.*

9. *Tom Hamilton, a Navy admiral, is the only Gold Medal winner who is also in as a player. Hamilton also coached the Navy team.*

10. *Stagg is the all-time winner as a college coach with 316 victories. That's one more than Glenn S. (Pop) Warner.*

11. *Rockne's "Win one for the Gipper" speech took five minutes.*

12. *Merlin Olsen first achieved Hall of Fame distinction by being selected as that institution's first scholar-athlete, which carries with it a stipend for ongoing education. Olsen is the first of these young men to return as a distinguished performer.*

13. *Don Whitmire, Navy tackle, was the admiral in charge of the Viet Nam evacuation.*

14. *Gus Zarnas, Ohio State guard who played in the late thirties, was born in Greece.*

15. *The only Hall of Famer born in Australia was Pat O'Dea, an astonishing kicker for Wisconsin before World War I. He was a master of that now-lost art, the dropkick, frequently connecting for shots of 60 yards.*

O'Dea's postcollege career was a strange one. He disappeared from his San Francisco home around 1917, and it was said that he had met a detachment of Australian troops on their way to the war in Europe and had joined them. Some time later an investigator discovered him living in southern California under the assumed name of "Mitchell." O'Dea's explanation was that his football fame interfered with his profession as a lawyer, and that things had worked out better under the anonymity of his assumed name.

16. *Adam Walsh, center of that team at Notre Dame, was also the captain. He went on to coach college and pro ball, including stints at Santa Clara, Yale, Harvard, and the Los Angeles Rams. Later he became a U.S. marshal in Maine.*

17. *Dick Van Sickle, a Florida end in the late twenties, was a Hollywood stunt man who died when his car skidded in a pool of oil.*

18. *Barney Poole played in an era when a relaxed attitude toward eligibility made it possible for him to have eight years of college ball, including playing as a freshman at Ole Miss. He also played for North Carolina Pre-Flight and for the U.S. Military Academy, and his collegiate career spanned the years 1941 through 1948. He later played pro ball for several clubs, winding up with the New York Giants.*

19. *Walter Camp was the first to pick the All-America team, selecting his first in 1889 and his last in 1924. He was a participant in* the first Yale–Harvard game, and for a while his "All-America team" ignored anyone who didn't play for the Big Three—Yale, Harvard, or Princeton. After a while he grudgingly took in more of the country, although he didn't reach the West Coast until he was just about finished.

20. Irvine (Cotton) Warburton, a Southern California back in the early thirties, won an Oscar for film editing on the movie Mary Poppins.

21. The "Vow Boys" got to three Rose Bowls, all that took place in the seasons in which most of them were eligible.

22. They won only one, losing to Columbia in 1934 and Alabama in 1935 before beating Southern Methodist in 1936.

23. The Vow Boys' Hall of Famers were Bobby Grayson and Bones Hamilton, backs; and Bill Corbus and Bob Reynolds, linemen.

24. In the All-Time Cotton Bowl backfield, Baugh was from Texas Christian, Layne from the University of Texas, Kimbrough from Texas A. and M., and Maegle from Rice.

25. Hall of Famer Brick Muller was the first All-America selected from a West Coast team.

26. Coaches in the Dartmouth–Cornell "5th Down" game were Red Blaik for Dartmouth and Carl Snavely for Cornell. The extra down given Cornell in that game remains the most famous of official boo-boos in the history of the sport. The uproar started the next day, and continued through the viewing of the films of the game. When it was evident that Cornell had scored its touchdown through a mistake by the referee, who is charged with keeping track of the downs, Cornell's president advised his Dartmouth counterpart that the decision was reverting to Dartmouth.

The official, W.H. (Red) Friesell, had a simple explanation for his misfeasance. "I missed it," he explained. Friesell was one of the best football officials in the east at the time. Asa S. Bushnell, Commissioner of the Eastern College Athletic Conference, sent him a buck-up telegram. "Don't let this get you down, down, down, down," it read.

Some Important College "Firsts"

What was

1. the first time a college coach was hung in effigy?
2. the first doctor with the title of "team physician"?
3. the first indoor football game?
4. the first regularly scheduled college football telecast?
5. the first coast-to-coast college football telecast?
6. the first intersectional college game?
7. the first time uniforms were worn in a game?
8. the first time helmets were worn?
9. the first time helmets were mandatory?
10. the first time numerals were required?
11. the first time both front and back numerals were required?

ANSWERS

1. *The first time that a college coach was hung in effigy was in 1893, and the poor fellow wasn't even a full-time coach. He was Lloyd Elliott, the captain and "acting" coach of the University of Iowa team that was upset by Grinnell, 36–14. Iowa supporters were so mad that when they got back home they stuffed a uniform with straw and strung it up on the telegraph wires down at the railroad station, explaining to everyone it was the Iowa captain-coach.*

2. *Dr. William Conant was the first team doctor, Harvard, 1890.*

3. *First indoor football game was played in Madison Square Garden in New York, in 1902. The players were college boys getting paid. A team representing Syracuse beat Philadelphia 6–0 in the final game, and the crowd was a slim one. Good thing, too, because the game might have gone indoors for good.*

4. *Fordham played Waynesburg in the first college football game telecast, on October 5, 1940.*

5. *The first college game to go coast-to-coast on TV was Illinois–Wisconsin, 1951.*

6. *Yale and Michigan played the first intersectional game in 1881. Yale won 17–0.*

7. *The first football uniforms were worn in 1875 in a Yale–Harvard game. Harvard won 4 goals to 0,–there is no record of which team was rated better dressed.*

8. *Helmets were worn for the first time in 1896. Before that headbands held long hair in place, or at least out of the players' eyes. The longer the hair the more protection it was supposed to provide.*

9. *In 1939, for the first time, you couldn't play without a helmet. Unbelievably there were a number of pro players who disdained head coverings of any kind. And at $200 a game, too.*

10. *They had been playing the game for almost a half century before people realized that you couldn't tell who the players were, even with a program. So in 1915 numbers were made mandatory.*

11. *In 1937 the college people figured that it wouldn't hurt and ordered identifying numbers, front and back.*

[104]

FOURTH QUARTER

Through These Portals...

The Pro Football Hall of Fame, the game's centerpiece and repository for its traditions, is located in Canton, Ohio, where the National Football League was formed more than sixty years ago. It was opened in 1963, with an initial group of seventeen inductees. That figure has gone well over one hundred, and the shrine has become an attraction for American fans as well as visitors from many foreign countries.

Each July, a Hall of Fame game between two National Football League teams serves as a counterpoint to the induction ceremonies that same day. A bust of each new man is exhibited for the first time, then is placed in a permanent niche in the special gallery housing all the previous inductees.

One of the features among the many displays is an electronic question-and-answer board that lights up if the correct answer is selected. There are eight questions, or rather descriptions, with the fan being asked to match one of eight corresponding Hall of Fame names. The descriptions follow:

1. He caught eighteen passes in one game.

2. He never played college football but starred in the pros.

3. He drop-kicked four field goals in one game.

4. He returned eight punts for touchdowns during his career.

5. He intercepted four passes in one game.

6. His two touchdown passes won the 1933 NFL title game.

7. He played in five College All-Star games.

8. He scored forty points in one NFL game.

ANSWERS

1. *Tom Fears, of the Los Angeles Rams, caught eighteen passes in one game against Green Bay in 1950. This record has withstood the onslaught of thirty years, including the early days of the American Football League, when several receivers topped one hundred receptions a season and others came close. Fears also coached the New Orleans Saints for five seasons. In Fears's era the Rams were alternating quarterbacks, and on his eventful afternoon he caught six thrown by Bob Waterfield and a dozen by Norm Van Brocklin. The game was played in Los Angeles, where gloves are not required equipment in early December.*

2. *Joe Perry never got to play beyond junior college ball at Compton, California. He entered the Navy, where he also played and was "discovered" by the 49ers. On leaving the service he picked the pros over a dozen college offers although, as he has said, some of the colleges "made better offers."*

3. *Dropkicking, now a forgotten art, was an alternate method of kicking field goals and extra points in the days when the ball was more rotund and kickable. Paddy Driscoll, who made the Hall of Fame as a 160-pound quarterback for the Chicago Cardinals and Chicago Bears, drop-kicked four of these for 23, 18, 50, and 35 yards against the Columbus Panhandles in 1925. Driscoll later was, for years, a member of George Halas's coaching board of strategy.*

4. *Jack Christiansen, a defensive back in 1951–58, the days of the Detroit Lions' greatest glory, and later coach of the 49ers, had eight lifetime punt returns for touchdowns, including four in his rookie year. He had two more the following year before the other teams started to get the idea and instructed their players not to punt in his direction.*

5. *Sammy Baugh is the player who first intercepted four times in a game, which is usually a shocker to those answering the quiz since Baugh is rated among the top five passers of all time. What was he doing intercepting someone else's passes? Baugh started playing in the single-platoon days; you played offense and when the other fellows got the ball you played defense. Sammy was a defensive back and one of the best. He led the NFL in 1943 with eleven in-*

[109]

terceptions, this in a ten-game schedule. His four-in-a-day came in that season against the Detroit Lions. It's been tied a half-dozen times but never topped.

6. *Bronko Nagurski's two passes won the 1933 NFL game over the New York Giants, another excellent example of the wrong man being in the right place. Nagurski was an awesome 240-pound fullback, and the opposition came to respect his bone-crushing proclivities. So George Halas developed a play in which big Bronko would fake a plunge, step back a pace, and lob a pass to an end cutting across the middle. The defenders, braced for the impact of an onrushing Nagurski, wouldn't be able to untrack themselves in time. Two of these fakes wound up as six-pointers in the 23–21 victory in the first game played between East and West in the NFL.*

7. *Charley Trippi, Chicago Cardinals halfback, played for the University of Georgia during World War II when eligibility rules were somewhat elastic. He got into the Chicago Tribune's since-departed All-Star game as a collegian in 1943, '44, '45, and '47, then came back as a member of the Cardinals who qualified for the 1948 game by having won the League championship. There have been numerous instances of a player making the game as a collegian one year and as a member of the championship pro team the next.*

8. *Ernie Nevers enjoyed pro football's biggest individual day in 1929 when he scored forty points for the Chicago Cardinals. These were all the points in the game except for the six scored by Garland Grange, Red Grange's brother, for the Chicago Bears' only score. Nevers scored six touchdowns and kicked four extra points. Two other players, Dub Jones, of Cleveland, in 1951, and Gayle Sayers, of the Bears, in 1965, each scored six touchdowns in a game but weren't involved in any extra-point efforts. O.J. Simpson, greatest ball carrier of the seventies, never came close to this achievement. In 1931, Nevers's last year with the Cardinals, he played in all nineteen games, including the ten exhibitions scheduled. In one, Nevers was knocked out and was unconscious for two minutes. Everyone on the field waited patiently until he recovered before resuming the game. The crown had paid its money to see Nevers.*

Did Anyone Get His Time?

Once considered a piece of sports equipment limited largely to track coaches and racetrack handicappers, the stopwatch is now a standard working item in football. It's used for everything from determining whether the game has run its full course to whether a player meets—or better, exceeds—minimum performance standards.

Into the game's lexicon has slipped such expressions as "two-minute game," "hang-time," etc. Here are several looks into this comparatively new area.

1. Who keeps the official time?

2. In a college game how much time is a team permitted for running off a play? In a pro game?

3. How many time-outs may each team have in college ball? In pro ball?

4. What actually is the "two-minute game," or "two-minute warning?"

5. What is rated a prime strategic move, offensively, in the two-minute game?

6. How about defensively?

7. What is a "commercial time out"?

8. Quarterbacks are rated on their ability to "get rid" of the ball as rapidly as possible. What does the coaching fraternity figure as a "safe time" for the quarterback to divest himself of ownership, before he risks getting ground into the turf?

[111]

9. "Hang time" is a comparatively recent addition to the working football vocabulary. What is it, and what are its varying degrees of success?

10. Pro clubs have always been tempted by world-class sprint men, even though these athletes' football knowledge or accomplishments may have been minimal. What sprint champion achieved the greatest success in the pros?

11. Football players are speed-tested over a 40-yard route. What is a good time for a back? A lineman?

12. It's a question whether football's protective gear is an impediment to speed. What is the fastest a player in standard garb including pads, cleats, and the rest, has been able to go?

ANSWERS

1. *Official time is kept by a scoreboard-clock operator. The line judge on the field also keeps the time on his own watch in the event there is a breakdown of the scoreboard clock.*

2. *The colleges allow 25 seconds for a play to be run off from the time the referee signals the ball in play. The pros have 30 seconds. Yes, there are more plays in a college game.*

3. *Both the pro and college games permit three time-outs per team in each half. They are carefully conserved against the time they might be needed to stop the clock late in each half.*

4. *The "two-minute warning" is a fixture of the pro game. The game is stopped two minutes from the end of each half to give the players notice of the time remaining. It doesn't have nearly the dramatic impact in the first half as in the second, where a club that is trailing by a field goal or by a touchdown may be driving. The colleges don't have a two-minute warning.*

5. *A segment of a week's preparation for all pro games is given over to the two-minute game, with offensive and defensive strategies planned. Offensively, a team must be prepared to run successive plays without using a huddle, thereby saving a half minute of the precious clock. Instead the quarterback calls successive plays in the preceding huddle.*

6. *Since the pass is generally rated the biggest single long-yardage weapon, the defense during the two-minute game concerns itself primarily with this threat. A fifth defensive back is inserted, usually at the expense of a linebacker or of moving a lineman back into a linebacker's spot. The opposing quarterback can usually complete a short pass against this type of defense, but the idea is to "give him the short stuff," hoping he won't get enough of these completions to add up to the first downs he needs. And then the receiver could always drop a short pass, too.*

7. *Televising the game makes it necessary to allot a definite number of time-outs for the commercial message to be perpetrated upon the viewer. Since the normal number of time-outs aren't enough, the "commercial" time-out was evolved. They are ar-*

ranged by the referee and the TV director. The idea is to have one when it least influences the flow of the game, i.e., try not to call a time-out when a team is driving on the 20-yard line.

8. *From the time the quarterback takes the ball from under the center he has about 4½ seconds to drop back 7 or 8 yards for the pass and divest himself of the pigskin. That would ordinarily be enough time if his prime passing target is open, but when he has to go to a secondary target, or possibly a third, it gets interesting. More than that 4½ seconds and he's stuck with the ball. With rare exceptions quarterbacks are taught not to run with the ball. Unless the player happens to be someone like a Fran Tarkenton, who has driven would-be assassins nuts, opposing linemen and linebackers like nothing better than having a crack at a running quarterback.*

9. *"Hang time" is the term applied to the length of time a punt stays in the air. The longer the better, because it permits members of the kicker's team to get to the spot where the ball will eventually descend. Ideally, they'd like to be there to shake hands with the would-be catcher. If hang time is 3.8 seconds, that's acceptable. Four seconds means you'll usually keep working for your owners until someone better comes along; 4.8 means you can have the job until you're old and gray.*

10. *World-class sprinters, Olympians, and others on that level have always been a temptation to the pros, but with rare exception they haven't worked out. The big exception was, of course, Bob Hayes, double sprint winner at the 1964 Olympics, who went on to a career with the Dallas Cowboys. Others who tried and failed were Tommie Smith and John Carlos. Henry Carr, another Olympic winner, was turned into a defensive back by the Giants.*

11. *Forty yards is the speed yardstick because a football player is rarely called upon to do something beyond that distance, (even though the field measures two-and-a-half times that.) A good clocking for a back or a receiver would be 4.5 seconds. Linemen, linebackers, etc. range from 4.8 to 5.0, and tight ends, with their larger bulk to go with their swiftness, are expected to do around 4.7. Defensive backs should register the same as running backs or receivers, 4.5. Sometimes they are called upon to do it backwards.*

12. *You can't run as fast with all that armament as you can in a pair of shorts and a shirt, but there have been some fellows who* *could turn it on, even when weighted down. Almost fifty years ago they clocked Frank Wykoff, a top sprinter who competed for Southern California, in 9-2/5 seconds, winning the national A.A.U. championship in ordinary running clothes. With football gear and leather cleats, he was only 1 second slower.*

The Tournament of Roses

The Rose Bowl, played in Pasadena, California every New Year's Day, is the oldest (1902) and biggest (102,000) of the postseason college football games. It was started originally as an added attraction to a rose festival staged by the local chamber of commerce to call attention to the salubrious midwinter climate in that section of California. Ironically, before the turn of the century California was LOOKING for people to settle there.)

The Rose Bowl has established a string of firsts, including its being the first sports event to be broadcast coast-to-coast. Its parade marshals have included presidents and Shirley Temple. Bob Hope made it twice. The format, considered a little restrictive by some, has the champion of the Pac-10 (formerly the Pacific Coast Conference) playing the winner in the Big Ten. Frequently, the theoretical national college championship is decided in one of the other major bowls, but the Rose Bowl people like the arrangement. Apparently, so do the Pac-10 and Big Ten, who stagger away from the party with an awesome check.

1. Why was there a fourteen-year break between the first Rose Bowl in 1902 and the next?

2. During that break, how did the natives amuse themselves on New Year's Day?

3. In 1925 Notre Dame beat Stanford, 27–10, even though Stanford outgained the Irish in virtually all departments. Pop Warner, Stanford coach, suggested that a new plan for scoring might be in order–points for first downs and yards gained, as well as scoring. What was Knute Rockne's response?

4. In 1929 Roy Riegels, of California, ran 64 yards the wrong way, setting up the safety that led to an 8–7 Alabama victory. It couldn't happen today on two counts. Why not?

5. What was the only unbeaten, untied, and unscored-upon team to play in the Rose Bowl, and how did it make out?

6. When did the Rose Bowl officials decide that it would be exclusively an intersectional rivalry between the Pac-10 and the Big Ten?

7. Many famous radio announcers have handled the Rose Bowl broadcasts. Four were also World Series announcers. Name them.

8. When the Rose Bowl was the undisputed top football event of the world (that honor has since passed along to the Super Bowl in terms of TV viewership, ticket demand, etc.), the distinction of having played in a Rose Bowl game and in a World Series was shared by two men. Who were they?

9. What Rose Bowl player appeared in three successive Rose Bowl games?

10. KF-79, the play that helped Columbia to beat heavily favored Stanford in 1934, was a spinner play off an unbalanced line. What was unusual about it?

ANSWERS

1. *In 1902 Michigan's point-a-minute team whacked Stanford, 49–0. The locals and the surrounding college teams lost interest in this kind of a show, and it wasn't revived until 1916. Brown University came out and was beaten by Washington State.*

2. *During the fourteen-year hiatus, the natives amused themselves with things like chariot races, tent pegging, and races between elephants and camels (let's see Jimmy the Greek handicap that one).*

3. *To Pop Warner's suggestion that first downs and yards gained be given some kind of a scoring value after his club had exceeded Notre Dame in both categories and lost the game, Knute Rockne replied that he'd agree when they started giving baseball victories to teams with most men left on base.*

4. *Roy Riegels couldn't run the wrong way today on two counts; the college rules prohibit picking up a fumble and advancing it, and, as a 170-pound center, he wouldn't be in the game in the first place.*

5. *Duke, unbeaten, untied, and unscored upon in 1939, came close to finishing the campaign with a Rose Bowl shutout, too; but a last-minute pass by Doyle Nave, a backup California quarterback, to Antelope Al Kreuger beat the Blue Devils, 7–3.*

6. *In 1947 the Rose Bowl decided to go with an established Pacific Coast-Big Ten format, getting away from the sometimes hectic last-minute bidding by the other major bowls for the available talent.*

7. *Mel Allen, Curt Gowdy, Lindsey Nelson, and Red Barber have handled Rose Bowl broadcasts as well as World Series. Others who have worked the game have been Jack Brickhouse, Tommy Harmon, Sam Balter, Chick Hearn, Braven Dyer, Bill Stern, Harry Wismer, and Bob Considine.*

8. *Jackie Jensen played for California in the 1949 Rose Bowl and appeared with the New York Yankees in the 1951 World Series. He also was voted Most Valuable Player in the American League when he played with the 1958 Red Sox. Chuck Essegian, also with Cali-*

fornia in the Rose Bowl, got two hits in three pinch-hit attempts for the Los Angeles Dodgers in the 1959 World Series with the Chicago White Sox.

9. *Bob (Horse) Reynolds set a record that will never be broken when he played every minute of Stanford's Rose Bowl games in 1934, 1935, 1936. The only game Stanford won was the last, when it beat Southern Methodist, 7–0. Reynolds, an Oklahoman, paid his way through school, later became an important broadcasting executive in southern California, and owned the Los Angeles Angels with Gene Autry. His nickname "Horse" traced to a prank in which some students concealed a horse in his dormitory room.*

10. *KF-79, Columbia's "secret" weapon, gave the Columbia quarterback Cliff Montgomery three options—keeping the ball, or handing it off to either of his halfbacks. He gave it to Al Barabas, who skirted left end for the game's only TD. Much was made of the "surprise" and "secret" aspects of this play. "Surprise," yes, "secret," no. Said Barabas in later years: "Some secret! Lou Little must have had us run that play 500 times in practice."*

Another Visit with the Greatest Stars in the Pro Game

We're back in Canton among the exhibits and memorabilia at the Pro Football Hall of Fame. Plenty of parking and up the road there's the country club where President William McKinley played golf.

Canton was an original member of the National Football League, and hung in there until 1926 when it became obvious that if pro football was going to make it, it wasn't going to be in a pick-up version of town ball with college kids playing under assumed names.

Today you can find cars with license plates from a dozen different states every afternoon in the Hall's parking lot. Canton has made it in pro football but in a manner completely different from that pictured by the men who backed the first team in the twenties.

1. What Pro Hall of Famer quit at the height of his career because the owner of his ball club refused to give him a raise?

2. The original group of seventeen inductees in 1963 included two coaches and two quarterbacks. Who were they?

3. Who is the only man in both the Baseball and Pro Football Halls of Fame?

[120]

4. Name the only two quarterbacks in the Hall of Fame who played together on the same team.

5. Who was the Hall of Famer who was the last to play both ways in the pros?

6. Who was the first player from the American Football League to be elected to the Hall of Fame?

7. Hugh (Shorty) Ray was a snappy 5'5" and weighed about 140 pounds. What was the basis of his election to the Hall of Fame?

8. There have been a half-dozen presidents and commissioners of the National Football League. How many are in the Hall?

9. One Hall of Fame member set a record for coaching the same club in three different time periods. Who was he?

10. Who is the only man not in the Hall of Fame for whom a deal was made involving an entire team?

11. Who is the only Hall of Famer to be born in Central America?

12. The Pro Football Hall of Fame offers six pairs of teammates, the first of which was Joe Guyon and Jim Thorpe in 1912 both from the Carlisle Indian School. Name the other five.

13. The original group of inductees in the Pro Hall of Fame numbered seventeen. In 1951, when the College Hall of Fame was set up, it included thirty-one charter members. There were nine cross-overs, meaning players who were in both first groups. Name them.

ANSWERS

1. *Cliff Battles, a Phi Beta Kappa, who was as tough as he was brainy, quit the Redskins and pro ball after he had enjoyed an 800-yards-plus season in 1937. The mercurial George P. Marshall, owner of the club, refused his request for a $1,500 raise, and Battles packed it in. He coached briefly, running the Brooklyn Dodgers in the All-America Football conference for a season and a half. He and Greasy Neale, who made it as a coach, give tiny West Virginia Wesleyan a representation in the Pro Football Hall of Fame.*

2. *Among the seventeen charter inductees were coaches George Halas and Curley Lambeau. The quarterbacks were Sammy Baugh and Earl (Dutch) Clark. Clark was a superstar despite poor vision that necessitated his wearing glasses off the field. There were no contact lenses fifty years ago.*

3. *Cal Hubbard, a giant lineman for Green Bay, New York, and Pittsburgh, is also in the Baseball Hall of Fame at Cooperstown. He made it as an umpire, one of perhaps a half dozen.*

4. *In the early 1950s the Los Angeles Rams came up with Norm Van Brocklin to back up Bob Waterfield. They were both so good that they were used alternately. Defensive backs used to have plenty of sleepless nights the week before playing the Rams. Waterfield finished up in '52, Van Brocklin went to '57 with the Rams before being traded to the Eagles, where he led them to a championship. Both Waterfield and Van Brocklin were talented beyond their passing; Waterfield led the league in field-goal kicking, and Van Brocklin enjoyed a similar eminence in the punting department.*

5. *Chuck Bednarik, center and linebacker for the Eagles into the early sixties, was the last of the 60-minute men.*

6. *First player from the American Football League to be elected to the Hall of Fame was Lance Alworth, who played nine years with the San Diego Chargers and finished up with Dallas. He caught 567 passes, lifetime, which places him among the top half dozen, all-time. Only Don Maynard compiled more yardage off almost a hundred additional catches.*

7. *Shorty Ray won his place in the Pro Hall of Fame by organiz-*

*ing the pro rules into their present from and clarifying the inter-
pretation of them.*

8. *Hall of Fame occupants among football league presidents and
commissioners include Joe Carr, who put the whole thing together
in 1921, and Bert Bell, who came up with the idea of the pension
plan and the telecasting of away games. (When Pete Rozelle is inducted, his bronze bust will be placed in a special niche, atop a TV
set.)*

9. *Walt Kiesling was a tough, stand-up tackle from the pioneer
days whose strong friendship with Art Rooney, the Pittsburgh
owner, kept him working in a head-coach capacity beyond the usual
scheme of things in pro ball. Once you're gone, you're gone, but in
Keese's case he had three shots: 1939–40, 1941–44, and 1954–56.
His last showing could just as well have been skipped, because he's
the one who cut a rookie named Johnny Unitas.*

10. *Benny Friedman, a Michigan All-America quarterback and a
powerful factor in the early success of the New York Giants, is a
lamentable omission from the Pro Hall of Fame. The Giants got him
by buying the entire Detroit Wolverines team and keeping only
Friedman and the Detroit coach, Leroy Andrews.*

11. *Steve Van Buren, of the Philadelphia Eagles, was born in
Honduras and was brought up in New Orleans by grandparents. He
scored seventy-one pro touchdowns and was strong enough to run
repeatedly at the right side of the line and fast enough to shake a
defensive back with his speed of 100 yards in 9.8 seconds.*

12. *The pairings in the Pro Football Hall of Fame, men who
played on the same college team, include Joe Guyon and Jim
Thorpe, from the Carlisle Indian School, 1912; Mel Hein and Turk
Edwards, Washington State, 1930; Vince Lombardi and Alex
Wojciechowicz, Fordham, 1935; Dante Lavelli and Bill Willis, Ohio
State, 1942; Art Donovan and Ernie Stautner, Boston College, 1949;
and Ollie Matson and Gino Marchetti, San Francisco, 1951.*

13. *"Cross-overs," meaning first picks for both the College and
Pro Halls of Fame, were Sammy Baugh, Dutch Clark, Red Grange,
Mel Hein, Fats Henry, Don Hutson, Bronko Nagurski, Ernie Nevers,
and Jim Thorpe.*

The Big Game

Football's founding fathers conceived the game originally as a pastime to take care of the Saturday afternoons roughly from shortly after Labor Day to some time before Christmas. January football, except for the college bowl stuff around New Year's Day, was in the same category as putting a man on the moon while his driver went sailing around it yodeling Christmas carols.

Now, thanks to the magic of television, a late January football game is (a) the biggest single sports event on the North American continent, (b) a disrupter of Sunday dinner for more than 100,000,000 people, and (c) an attraction for the cream of the nation's pickpockets, forcing them to leave home for a week to make a half-year's income (not reportable to the IRS) in whatever warm-weather city the Super Bowl is being played. Jammed stadium entrances before and after the game are a grifter's dream. Crowded elevators at the hotels in town aren't bad either. The Super Bowl itself was no particular person's dream. Shortly after the American Football League came into being in 1960, it challenged the National Football League to a post-season game to decide the world championship. It was told to go scratch. Six years later, when the two leagues merged so as to stop cutting each other's throats, things were different and the first game between the two leagues was hastily put together. It was played at the end of the 1966 season, in January 1967.

It wasn't called the "Super Bowl," then, but was billed by the cumbersome title of "AFL-NFL World Championship Game," a tag that lasted a couple of years. That Roman numeral stuff came in after a while and stuck despite attempts by some to junk it with lines like, "A XVII-pt. underdog? No way is Baltimore that much better than the Jets. I'm sending in IIIM on the Jets. And it's XI to V in man-to-man betting."

[124]

1. Where did the name "Super Bowl" come from?

2. Where was the first Super Bowl game played, and how successful was it?

3. What was the first Super Bowl that the American Football League (later Conference) won?

4. What was the first Super Bowl game in which two "expansion" teams played?

5. Who was the first player to win four Super Bowl championship rings?

6. Unlike baseball, where a World Series share depends on the gates of the first four games, Super Bowl performers get a flat fee for winning or losing. What are the payments?

7. Acting as referee on the team of officials at the Super Bowl is regarded as the No.-1 plum in the business. Two men have been picked three times. Who are they?

8. Only two men, both quarterbacks, have been named MVP twice in Super Bowl competition. Who are they?

9. Franco Harris's 158 yards rushing, set in 1975, is a single-game record in the Super Bowl. Whose previous record did he break?

10. Has a left-handed passer ever led a team to a Super Bowl victory?

11. The Super Bowl was conceived as a warm-weather attraction and has been played variously in southern California, New Orleans, Houston, and Miami. What broke the sun-belt string?

12. Has the MVP award in the Super Bowl ever gone to a player on a losing team?

13. Minnesota holds the record for being in four losing Super Bowl efforts. Fran Tarkenton was the quarterback in three.

Who was the other starting quarterback, and who replaced him when he was injured late in the game?

14. The Super Bowl is regarded as the "hottest" ticket in American sport, meaning it's the most highly regarded and sought after. In one Super Bowl tickets literally went begging. Which one?

15. In Super Bowl VII, Miami was leading Washington by a nice two-touchdown margin when an untoward event occurred that made the outcome uncomfortably close for the Dolphins. What was it?

16. What Super Bowl was decided in the final 9 seconds?

17. What Super Bowl winner was cheered on by 80,000 fans waving handkerchiefs?

18. And which group a few years later used towels?

19. Who said, "Let's not look at the movies, we might become too confident"?

20. Max McGee went out on a tremendous note of victory in Super Bowl I. What were the circumstances?

ANSWERS

1. *Lots of people take credit for this one. Actually, it was Lamar Hunt's young son, playing with a toy ball called a "Super Ball," who did it. The idea of "AFL-NFL World Championship Game" was driving everyone nuts, and besides there wouldn't be any AFL shortly. Lamar Hunt looked at his boy's toy, patted him on the head, and called his confreres telling them that the name for the game was now taken care of.*

2. *The first Super Bowl (see "AFL-NFL World Championship Game") was played in the Los Angeles Coliseum, which was only two-thirds filled. Green Bay vs. Kansas City didn't have much of an appeal for the Californians. Special trips to the game were still off into the future.*

3. *The third game, Jets vs. Colts, was the American Football League's first victory. And in good time, too. There was a considerable faction in the newer league afraid of the one-sided aspects of the first two Green Bay victories, and they were suggesting that the game be eliminated.*

4. *Dallas beat Miami in Super Bowl VI, in New Orleans, and this marked the first clash of "expansion" teams in the post-season championship.*

5. *Marv Fleming, a tight end who began with Green Bay and finished playing for Miami, picked up two rings with each of these clubs in Super Bowls. He posed with all four, with only his thumb uncovered. It was real funny looking.*

6. *Each man on the winning team gets $18,000, losers $9,000. Officials get $1,500 no matter what position they work and are picked on the basis of the quality of their performance during the season just past. It costs in the vicinity of a million dollars to put on the game, but if you multiply 100,000 seats times thirty dollars, and tack on another four or five million for TV, there's a comfortable margin for profit.*

7. *Norm Schachter and Jim Tunney, both Californians, have been selected as referees for three Super Bowls.*

8. *MVP honors in the Super Bowl have gone twice to Bart Starr,*

[127]

with Green Bay, who enjoyed the honor first, and Pittsburgh's Terry Bradshaw.

9. Franco Harris's Super Bowl rushing record of 158 yards broke a record of 145 yards set by Miami's Larry Csonka in Super Bowl VIII.

10. When Oakland won Super Bowl XII, Ken Stabler, a left-hander, was at the helm. He enjoyed a comparatively easy triumph over Minnesota.

11. The NFL voted to hold the 1982 Super Bowl game (after the 1981 season) in the Pontiac (Michigan) Silverdome, a covered job that houses 80,000. Political considerations played a part here.

12. Chuck Howley, Dallas linebacker, was voted the MVP award in Super Bowl V, when the Cowboys lost to Baltimore.

13. In Super Bowl IV the Kansas City Chiefs worked Minnesota's Joe Kapp over rather thoroughly, forcing him out of the game in the fourth quarter. His place was taken by Gary Cuozzo, once a back-up quarterback behind Johnny Unitas at Baltimore.

14. In Super Bowl I, played in Los Angeles, the game was a tough sell and the radio and newspapers carried day-of-the-game ads telling of the availability of good seats. The two television networks carried the game simultaneously, which didn't help the gate, either. But after that, the games became a scalper's dream.

15. Garo Yepremian, one of the great kickers the game has known, found himself in an unusual and unwanted role in Super Bowl VIII. He was attempting a field goal to add to Miami's comfortable 14-0 lead and it was blocked. Yepremian picked it up and—horrors—tried to pass it. It wobbled into the hands of Washington defensive back Mike Bass, who went half the field with it for a touchdown, which suddenly made a game of it. Miami managed to win, and Yepremian never tried another pass.

16. Super Bowl V, Baltimore over Dallas, was decided in the last 9 seconds on Jim O'Brien's successful field goal from in close. Baltimore killed the clock until there was little chance of Dallas coming back after the three-pointer—standard procedure.

17. Miami fans came up with the waving handkerchiefs idea.

18. *Later, Pittsburgh was waved on by the "Terrible Towels," a more colorful display—they were all yellow.*

19. *The Jets, led by the sagacious little Weeb Ewbank, spotted plenty on the Colts' films they examined (a perfectly legal thing to do) before Super Bowl III. Joe Namath is supposed to have made the crack about not become over confident, but let's give it to Ewbank, where it belongs. What the Jets spotted was a weakness in the Colts' defensive line. Two of their starting front four never played another game.*

20. *Max McGee was coming to the end of a career as a receiver with the Packers in the first Super Bowl. That season he had caught only two passes. Then Boyd Dowler, the starter, was hurt and McGee had a big afternoon in which he caught seven passes, two for touchdowns.*

Man with the Whistle

They're sometimes called "zebras," because of the striped black-and-white shirts they wear. They're dressed like old-fashioned golfers in knickers and white caps. And they're just as proud of their ability to run a game as the men who are playing it. Every so often one of them winds up in the hospital with a broken leg or worse, bringing the realization that it's no picnic out there among a mass of several tons of charging, slamming humanity.

Without them there could be no game; with them the main yardstick is their anonymity. The less you're aware of football officials, the better the game they're running. Here are a few looks at the men whose own families are often the only friends they have in the stadium.

1. Of all the officials working a game, who commands the highest rate of pay?

2. The pros went to a total of seven officials to a game a couple of years ago, adding a "side judge". What are the other six positions?

3. What game official occupies the riskiest position?

4. Coaches and club owners watch all officials, but why do they watch the referee more closely than others?

5. In the NFL, what official had the record for the longest number of years worked?

6. What was unusual about the assignment of officials for the first Super Bowl?

7. How many NFL officials are former pro players?

ANSWERS

1. *All NFL officials are paid the same amount, with seniority providing the difference in their pay checks: The longer a man has worked, the larger amount he'll get.*

2. *The officiating team consists of referee, umpire, head linesman, line judge, back judge, side judge, and field judge. The referee is in charge of the crew and the spokesman in any discussions, on the field or off.*

3. *The role of the umpire is considered the most risky among the official positions, because he is in the line of the developing play and must have a strong sense of anticipation. There's no law that says he, along with the defense, can't be fooled by some trick play and wind up at the bottom of a pile of players. Incidentally, if an official "spoils" a play, i.e., gets in the way of an obvious block or a pass reception, there's no recourse for anyone. (He'd better not do it too often, however.)*

4. *The referee's main responsibility, once the offense has developed its play, is to watch the quarterback, which loosely translates into "protecting" the quarterback. The idea is to prevent his being damaged via a cheap shot after he's gotten rid of the ball. "Roughing the passer" calls for a 15-yard penalty, which serves as a strong deterrent.*

5. *Dan Tehan, a retired Cincinnati sheriff, holds the record for having worked longest as an NFL official, serving thirty-four years, mostly as a head linesman or a back judge. He worked the first interdivisional title game in the league, the 1933 Bears–Giants game, and also the 1963 title game between these same two teams.,*

6. *The unusual aspect of the assignment of officials at the first Super Bowl game, after the 1966 season, was that each league, American and National, picked its six top men. Three from each side were selected to work the game and the others served as alternates. None of the alternates got into the game.*

7. *Ten of the current pro officials are former pro players. They*

*include Leo Miles, Lou Palazzi, and Pat Knight, all of the New York
Giants; Fred Wyant of the Redskins; Frank Sinkwich of the Lions;
Royal Cathcart of the 49ers; Al Conway of the Eagles; Ron Botchan
of the Chargers; Dean Look of the New York Titans; and Pat Harder
of the Chicago Cardinals.*

Loose Ends and Monday-Morning Quarterbacks

Have we forgotten anything? Your favorite player, perhaps, your favorite team, your favorite game? Maybe you'll find it here on this "poo-poo platter," which is Chinese-restaurant parlance for "a little bit of everything". And if we've missed—well, we've given it our best shot.

If you've caught us in a mistake somewhere along the line, save the sarcasm and scorn for more appropriate targets, like the politician who promises tax relief or the plumber who has to come back a third time to fix a leaky faucet.

Remember the line by the late Frank Menke, who devoted the latter part of his life to compiling and refining his *Encyclopedia of Sports.* Menke followed a long road all the way from (A) Angling to (Y) Yachting. Inevitably, he committed an occasional error and inevitably there was the comma-chaser out there to pick him up on it. Menke's answer to him was a "thank you" for calling it to his attention and then a suggestion . . . "I'll pay you five dollars for every error you find in the *Encyclopedia* if you'll pay me five cents for every item that's accurate." He got no takers.

[134]

THE PLAYERS

1. Weeb Ewbank has won a Super Bowl, but so have a half dozen other coaches. What's Weeb done that no one has accomplished in his line of work, and no one can ever duplicate?

2. Place kickers from foreign lands in the NFL are no novelty. Among the leaders have been Jan Stenerud and Garo Yepremian. What were their native lands?

3. At the height of his career as a rusher with the Miami Dolphins, Larry Csonka was tagged with the nickname "Butch Cassidy," from the movie starring Paul Newman and Robert Redford, *Butch Cassidy and the Sundance Kid*. Who was the Dolphins' "Sundance Kid," who ran alongside Csonka?

4. Who were the pro passers besides Y.A. Tittle, to complete seven touchdown tosses in a game? There are four.

5. Who is the all-time top pass receiver in number of passes caught? In yardage gained?

6. Two men have caught 100 or more passes in a season. Name them.

7. Dan Abramowicz played with the New Orleans Saints and the San Francisco 49ers, but never played in a postseason game with either team. What significant feat did he accomplish in pro football?

8. In the early days of professional football, pro wrestling used to be a handy means for football stars to augment their incomes. Players like Bronko Nagurski, Gus Sonnenberg, Sammy Stein, and others toured the circuit. Who was the last first-class player to wrestle professionally?

9. What is the record among rushers for the most consecutive games in which they scored one or more touchdowns?

10. In what movie did Pat O'Brien play the role of Knute Rockne?

11. Who portrayed the dying Notre Dame star, George Gipp, in that picture?

12. In the movie *Jim Thorpe, All-American*, who played Thorpe?

13. The National Football League instituted the draft in 1936. Who was the first No.-1 pick to make the Hall of Fame?

14. Has there ever been an instance of a major league commissioner of one season switching to the role of head coach in the next?

15. Among the football commissioners past and present, or among the commissioners in any other sport, only one holds the Congressional Medal of Honor. Who is he?

16. Jim Brown is the only rusher to win the NFL crown five years in a row. Who was the first to win it three times in a row?

17. Clark Shaughnessy, master of the T-formation, introduced the three-end offense in October 1949, when he was the coach of the Los Angeles Rams. Two of the ends were Hall of Famers Tom Fears and Elroy Hirsch. Who was the third man?

18. In the ten years of the American Football League's existence, one player was named to every All-League team. Who was he?

19. Norm Van Brocklin set the all-time single-game passing mark of 554 yards playing with the Los Angeles Rams. What was the opposing team?

20. Charley Hennigan set the pro record for 101 pass receptions in 1964. What team did he play for, and who was the quarterback?

21. When the NFL started keeping statistics in 1932, the scoring title went to a player who tallied thirty-nine points. Who was he?

22. The record for extra points kicked in one game is nine, shared by two players. Bob Waterfield of the Los Angeles Rams is one. Who is the other player, and in what capacity is he involved in football today?

23. In 1965 the Baltimore Colts were handicapped in their Western Conference play-off with Green Bay by the fact that both their starting quarterback and his backup had been injured shortly before the game. Tom Matte, with no pro experience, was pressed into service, with the plays written on his wristband. The sidelined regular quarterback was Johnny Unitas. Who was the other injured quarterback?

24. This passer piled up enough successful yardage to make a couple of round trips between downtown Minneapolis and neighboring St. Paul. Who was he?

25. And this one set a record of one or more touchdown passes in forty-seven consecutive games. Name him.

26. Sammy Baugh was an all-around athlete at Texas Christian University and at one time rated himself a better baseball player than a football player. What baseball organization signed him?

27. Who was it of whom Doak Walker, famed Lions running back of the fifties, said "He never lost a game; sometimes time just ran out on him"?

28. What football player's career extended over four decades?

29. Paul Brown's coaching career included high school, college, and armed forces teams and *three* major pro football leagues. Name the college and the three pro loops.

30. In the 1952 Yale–Harvard game, Yale's final extra point was caught by a player not on the official program. Who was he?

31. In 1954 Dick Moegle, a Rice back, bent on a 95-year run for touchdown, was brought down by an Alabama tackler who rewrote the rules by coming off the bench, bareheaded, just long enough to make a tackle at the 38-yard line. What was the officials' ruling on the play?

32. Wayne Millner, Redskins end, is a Hall of Famer, but is remembered by more people for a particular college feat than for his subsequent efforts in the money ranks. What was it?

33. What Super Bowl kicker made an off-season living diving for abalone off the Pacific coast in his native California?

34. Who is the only coach to have handled a major college football team and a major league baseball team?

35. In the 1956 draft Jim Brown was the *fifth* man selected. Who was picked before him?

36. Among pro owners, who besides George Halas has played pro ball?

37. Among winning Super Bowl coaches, who played pro ball?

38. Who was the only college runner to rush with the ball more than a thousand times?

39. What pro rusher carried the ball more times than anyone else?

40. Among top-line college coaches, who has the best won-lost percentage?

41. In 1941 Aldo (Buff) Donelli did a moonlighting coaching job that is absolutely unbelievable today. What was his double duty?

42. In thirty-five years, only one rookie has led the NFL in passing. Who was he?

43. Artie Donovan, Colts defensive lineman of the fifties, was a third-generation sports headliner. His father, Arthur Donovan, was a famous fight referee who worked most of Joe Louis's bouts. What was his grandfather famous for?

44. Usually the fact that a player is traded more than once doesn't look so good for him. But this one played in Super Bowls with three different teams. Who was he?

45. Who holds the record in the NFL for most scoring by a rookie?

46. When Walter Payton rushed for 275 yards in a game against Minnesota in 1977, he broke O.J. Simpson's single-game record. By how much?

47. The "umbrella defense" of more than a quarter century ago was a New York Giants innovation, with the defensive backs lining up roughly in the shape of an umbrella. One of the backs later became a winning Super Bowl coach. Name him.

48. Four NFL quarterbacks are in the books with 99-yard passes. Name them.

ANSWERS

1. *Weeb Ewbank won NFL championships in 1958 and 1959 with the Baltimore Colts and the AFL championship in 1968 with the New York Jets. It had never been done previously. With only one major league today, it couldn't happen again.*

2. *Jan Stenerud of the Kansas City Chiefs is Norwegian. Garo Yepremian is a native of Cyprus, who speaks four languages and kicks left-footed, soccer style.*

3. *The "Sundance Kid" to Larry Csonka's "Butch Cassidy" in the Super Bowl championship era in Miami was Jim Kiick, a sturdy halfback whose father had played pro ball for the Steelers.*

4. *Sid Luckman, Adrian Burk, Joe Kapp and George Blanda were the other passers who pegged seven six-pointers in a game. Blanda could probably have easily topped that figure if he'd played the entire game in the early-sixties rout of the New York Titans by the Houston Oilers; he came out shortly after the start of the second half.*

5. *The all-time pass receiver in number of passes caught is Charley Taylor, who caught 649 playing with Washington from 1964 to 1975 plus an additional season in 1977. Don Maynard, of the Jets, gained the most yardage among the receivers with 11,834—1,500 yards more than his closest rival.*

6. *Charley Hennigan, of Houston, with 101, and Lionel Taylor, of Denver, with an even 100, are the only two receivers to reach or top 100 receptions in a season. Taylor later coached the Steelers' receivers.*

7. *Dan Abramowicz, of the New Orleans Saints, caught at least one pass in each of 105 consecutive games.*

8. *Ernie Ladd, a gigantic defensive lineman with Kansas City, decided there was more money in pro wrestling than in pro football and went into the business of airplane spins and double hammerlocks. Wahoo McDaniel, an early Jet, also got into the racket, but he wasn't championship material and once they got over being impressed by his fancy nickname (his real name was Ed. He was part*

Choctaw and had played for Oklahoma), they found he was no Strangler Lewis.

9. *Lenny Moore, of the Baltimore Colts, holds the record for having rushed for one or more touchdowns in eleven successive games.*

10. *Pat O'Brien played the role of Knute Rockne in the movie* Knute Rockne, All-American.

11. *The role of George Gipp, the Notre Dame player who died tragically young of pneumonia, was played by Ronald Reagan.*

12. *In the Jim Thorpe movie, Burt Lancaster played the great American Indian athlete.*

13. *Bill Dudley, picked by Pittsburgh in 1942, was the first No.-1 first-round draft pick to make the Hall of Fame.*

14. *When the All-America Football Conference got going in 1946, Jim Crowley, one of the famed Four Horsemen of Notre Dame, was named commissioner. He didn't last past the first few weeks, when he was replaced by Jonas Ingram, a former admiral in the U.S. Navy. The following year Crowley was named coach of the Chicago Rockets, the team that had the unfortunate chore of challenging the Chicago Bears, the best team in football.*

15. *Joe Foss, first commissioner of the American Football League, was a Marine Corps fighter pilot who rose to the rank of general and won the Congressional Medal of Honor for action in the Pacific in World War II.*

16. *Jim Brown is the rusher with five straight NFL crowns. Before him, Steve Van Buren, of the Eagles, won it three straight times.*

17. *The third man in Clark Shaughnessy's three-end offense with the Los Angeles Rams in 1949 was Bob Shaw.*

18. *In the ten years of the American Football League, Oakland's center, Jim Otto, made All-League every season. Nineteen players finished with ten full years of AFL service, including Jack Kemp.*

19. *When Norm Van Brocklin passed for a record 554 yards, his 1951 Rams team was playing the New York Yanks. In Los Angeles.*

20. *Charley Hennigan's record of 101 pass receptions was set with the Houston Oilers. George Blanda was the quarterback.*

21. *In 1932, the first year that statistics were kept in the NFL, Dutch Clark of the Portsmouth Spartans led all scorers with thirty-nine points.*

22. *Bob Waterfield shares the record of nine extra points in one game with Pat Harder, former Cardinal, who is a league official today.*

23. *When the Baltimore Colts ran into all that quarterback trouble in 1965, the backup quarterback, also hurt after John Unitas's injury, was Gary Cuozzo.*

24. *The passing yardage record is held by Fran Tarkenton, who has approximately twenty-seven miles' worth of passing to his credit. John Unitas, whose record he broke, has twenty-three miles.*

25. *Unitas holds the record for forty-seven consecutive games with one or more touchdown passes. Raymond Berry, Jim Mutscheller, and Lenny Moore did most of the receiving.*

26. *Sammy Baugh was a good enough baseball player to be signed by the St. Louis Cardinals. He decided to stick with football when it became obvious he couldn't hit the curve too well.*

27. *The line "He never lost a game; sometimes time just ran out on him" referred to Bobby Layne. He was also the last quarterback to operate without a protective face guard. Hardly ever bothered tightening his shoelaces, either.*

28. *George Blanda's career spanned four decades, starting with the Bears late in the forties and reaching into the seventies.*

29. *Paul Brown coached at Ohio State. His three coaching roles in different pro leagues include the Cleveland Browns in the All-America Conference, the Browns in the NFL after the merger, the Cincinnati Bengals in the American Football League, and the Bengals again when the AFL was merged into the National Football League. That's a lot of leagues.*

30. *Yale was putting the final touches to a pretty good wacking of Harvard in their annual clash in 1952, so for the final extra point to make it a 41–14 victory, the Elis sent in their student manager. He caught the pass.*

31. *When that Alabama bench-warmer tacked Dick Moegle, the*

Rice star, en route to the goal line, the officials awarded Rice the touchdown anyway. Moegle had four that afternoon.

32. *Wayne Millner caught a late pass in a Notre Dame–Ohio State game back in the thirties that meant victory for the Irish. Oldsters still talk about it.*

33. *Jim Turner, who kicked for the Jets in Super Bowl III, is an experienced abalone diver in California. He also holds the record for field goals with thirty-four in one season.*

34. *Bezdek coached the Penn State football team, and later managed the Pittsburgh Pirates.*

35. *Here is how the draft went when Jim Brown was picked fifth: Bonus pick, Paul Hornung, Green Bay; No. 1, John Brodie, San Francisco; No. 2, Ron Kramer, Green Bay; No. 3, Len Dawson, Pittsburgh, and then No. 4, Jim Brown, Cleveland.*

36. *George Halas was a playing-owner when he helped pioneer the National Football League. No other current owner ever played pro, although Bud Adams and Lamar Hunt were college players. Art Rooney, of the Steelers, played with a fast semipro club called Hope-Harvey (Hope for the name of the firehouse in the district, Harvey for the name of the doctor who used to do the postgame patch-ups). They played teams like Canton in the early days, but they were never officially a member of the NFL.*

37. *A half-dozen Super Bowl coaches—Tom Landry, Bud Grant, Don McCafferty, Chuck Noll, Don Shula, and John Rauch—all played pro ball. Landry, McCafferty, Noll, and Shula were winners in the big one. Grant had four shots without success. Rauch was coach of the first Oakland team that lost in the Super Bowl. John Madden, coach of the winning Oakland club in a later Super Bowl, was prevented from playing by a knee injury after he had been signed by the Eagles.*

38. *Tony Dorsett, of Pittsburgh, is the only college runner to carry the ball more than 1,000 times in his career. He did it 1,074 times for a career 6,082 yards.*

39. *Jim Brown is the all-time ball carrier with 2,359 carries in nine years with the Cleveland Browns. It was enough to give him a career yardage record that has stood for fifteen years.*

40. *Knute Rockne's thirteen years at Notre Dame produced an incredible record of 105 victories, 12 defeats, 5 ties, for an average of .881. Next best was another Notre Dame coach, Frank Leahy. In, again, thirteen seasons that included a stint at Boston College, Leahy had a record of 107–13–9 for .864. Not much to choose from there.*

41. *Buff Donelli was a standout performer for Duquesne who came back to coach his alma mater. In 1941 the Pittsburgh pro job opened, and he took it as a part-time proposition. Elmer Layden, his former college coach, now commissioner of the NFL, told him he had to make a choice, and Donelli kept the college job. Later in his career he coached the Cleveland Rams, then returned to the college scene with Boston University and Columbia. As an athlete, he had once also kicked a goal for the United States in World Cup soccer.*

42. *Greg Cook, of the 1969 Cincinnati Bengals, was the last rookie to lead the NFL in passing. He developed a sore arm shortly thereafter and dropped out after a season or two.*

43. *Artie Donovan's grandfather, Mike, was middleweight boxing champion back in the 1880s. He seconded Jake Kilrain in the last bare-knuckle heavyweight championship fight with John L. Sullivan in 1889.*

44. *Preston Pearson played for Baltimore, Pittsburgh, and Dallas in Super Bowl games. He was a twelfth-round draft choice by Baltimore out of Illinois, where he didn't play football but made the basketball team as a nonscholarship player.*

45. *The NFL's rookie scoring record was set by Chicago's Gale Sayers in 1965 with 132 points.*

46. *Walter Payton's record 275 yards in one game broke the previous mark by O.J. Simpson by 2 yards.*

47. *Tom Landry was a member of the New York Giants' "umbrella defense" under Steve Owen. Others tried to copy the formation, more or less successfully.*

48. *The four NFL passers with 99-yard passes to their credit in the record books are: Frank Filchock (1939), George Izo (1963), Karl Sweetan (1966), and Sonny Jurgensen (1968). There is no breakdown of how much was pass and how much was run in each case.*

THE TEAMS AND THE GAMES

1. What was the first "expansion" team (one that was not an original member of either the American or the National League) to win a Super Bowl victory?

2. Candlestick Park in San Francisco has been the home of two professional football teams. Name them.

3. The Chicago Bears are generally regarded as having dominated the early and middle years of the pro game. Surprisingly, another team has won more championships. What team is that?

4. The uprights in the pro game are 30 feet high, about twice the height of those used in college ball. Why?

5. When the American Football League started up in the 1960 season, the eight AFL teams included rivals of the NFL in Los Angeles and Dallas. Subsequent moves placed these teams in which other cities?

6. Among current pro owners, who had to wait longest for a winner?

7. Only one team has ever won successive NFL championships by shutouts. Which one?

8. What was the first pro football team to go to training camp?

9. During World War II, when talent became in short supply, the Pittsburgh Steelers were combined with another team in two successive years. Name the two teams.

10. In 1933, in addition to East–West play-offs for the title being held for the first time, two important rule changes affected the structure of the pro game. What were they?

11. The 1967 Dallas–Green Bay championship game was played in weather that reached 13° *below* zero. That was admittedly pretty brisk, but it's not the cold-weather record for a football game. What is?

12. "The Foolish Club" was the nickname given to the original group of owners who banded together to form the American Football League in 1960. Why?

13. Since the start of the NFL in 1920, one city has maintained an unbroken association with it. What city is this?

14. How many pro football teams have gone through a season unbeaten?

15. In championship play, the scoring record is the seventy-three points racked up by the Chicago Bears over the Redskins in 1940. What is the second highest total?

16. What NFL championship game has no official records, statistics, or play-by-play?

17. Which of the NFL's twenty-eight teams is publicly owned?

18. If a kick hits the crossbar and goes over, it's good. But what happens if a passer, back in his end zone, hits the crossbar with the ball and it bounces back into the end zone, where the opposition then falls on it?

19. Who was the last pro player to compete without a face mask?

20. Which was the first club to use decorated helmets?

21. The AFL and NFL got together for the first time in the 1967 preseason. Who played in and who won the first game?

22. When was coaching from the bench legalized?

23. A "drive-train" injury is one of the mishaps that brings a frown to the face of the doctor who treats football players. What is it?

24. Football was the first sport to use scouting combines where clubs share the costs and benefit from the pooled information. Today there are three in operation. Name them.

25. What is the only pro major league club *not* a member of a scouting pool?

26. Since all the clubs in a pool get the same scouting information, what determines which club picks which candidate?

27. Which was the first college team to use the two-platoon system?

28. Georgia Tech set a record for cruel and unusual punishment with its 222–0 victory over the team of a small school called Cumberland in 1916. What was the most one-sided victory by a team over a major opponent?

29. A tie is like kissing the tax collector. What college holds the record for most deadlocks in one season?

30. While we're still among the ties, what was the highest tie score between two major opponents?

31. The number of yards gained from scrimmage is usually a pretty good sign of one team's superiority over another. What is the record for yards gained in scrimmage without scoring a touchdown in the game?

32. What midwestern university is rightfully called "The Cradle of Championship Coaches"?

33. Names on the backs of jerseys came in with the American Football League in 1960. When were numbers first introduced?

34. The dropkick was at one time the standard manner of scoring the extra point. The ball was held and dropped so as to bounce up in a way that let the kicker get his toe to it on the rise. The dropkick is still permitted, but what was the last time one was made in the NFL?

35. In sports medicine, what is the "rotator cuff"?

36. Unusual trades have been known to have taken place in football, including some where one of the more slippery coaches traded draft choices they didn't own. But what is the only time that two teams traded owners?

37. The World Football League, which managed to get 2,000 miles off the Continental United States with a team in Hawaii, was the last challenge to the National Football League. It went bust after a full season, with a brief cooperative profit-sharing sortie into the following September. It played one championship game. What was the outcome of that game?

38. The numbering system in pro ball was adopted in 1973, with the following allotments: 1–19, kickers and quarterbacks; 20–49, backs; 50–59, centers and linebackers; 60–79, defensive linemen and interior offensive linemen; 80–89, wide receivers and tight ends; 90–99, further defensive linemen. There are still some linebackers around with numbers like 10 and receivers with numbers in the teens. Why?

39. The argument of artificial turf vs. the natural stuff will continue as long as the game is played. Maintenance on the artificial surface is a lot cheaper, but what are some of the arguments against playing football on a "rug"?

40. What was the greatest number of head coaching changes on one NFL club within a 24-hour period?

41. What was the first coast-to-coast radio (radio, *not* television) broadcast of a pro football game?

ANSWERS

1. *The first expansion team to win the Super Bowl was Dallas, which beat Miami in Super Bowl VI. Dallas was an expansion team in the early sixties. Miami was an expansion team, too, in the American Football League, and the Dolphins' claim to fame is having been the first expansion team to win the Super Bowl twice.*

2. *Candlestick Park, built originally for the baseball Giants after they had moved to San Francisco from New York, is now the home of the 49ers, as well. A year or two after the Oakland Raiders came into being, they tried Candlestick but gave it up for a recreational facility in Oakland while their own stadium in Alameda County was being built.*

3. *Green Bay has won more championships than any other team—eleven to the Bears' eight. They are also a holdover from the days when NFL teams were really "town" teams. Green Bay's population is barely 100,000. Several home games each season are played in Milwaukee.*

4. *The uprights in pro ball, like those in college, used to be 10 feet high. In the 1965 Western Conference play-off between Baltimore and Green Bay, with Green Bay trailing by three points, they tried a field goal which Don Chandler missed. An official ruled it was good, tying the score. In overtime Chandler kicked one that was really good, and Green Bay went on to win the Conference title and then the NFL crown, beating Cleveland and Jimmy Brown in his last game.*
The following year, the uprights were very quietly boosted 10 feet, and a couple of years later another 10 feet were added. Thirty-foot uprights look a little awkward, but they help officials on a difficult call.

5. *After the AFL went into business it was obvious that neither Los Angeles nor Dallas would be able to support two pro teams in rival leagues. After a year, the Los Angeles Chargers moved to San Diego, and after two more seasons the Dallas Texans packed it in and moved to Kansas City, leaving the area to the Cowboys. When the AFL was being organized, Minneapolis was supposed to be a* charter member but defected to the NFL, so a franchise was hastily awarded to Oakland.

6. Art Rooney is generally regarded as the most patient person in sports. He bought an NFL franchise in 1933 and didn't have a winner until Super Bowl IX in 1975.

7. The Philadelphia Eagles won the 1948 NFL championship from the Cardinals, 7–0, and the 1949 title from the Rams, 14–0.

8. The Chicago Cardinals were the first team to go to training camp. The year was 1929, the place Coldwater, Michigan.

9. The Steelers combined with the Eagles in 1943 to form a team called the "Steagles". The following year the Steelers combined with the Chicago Cards. The two different combined teams won a total of five games.

10. In 1933 the pros made it permissible to pass from anywhere behind the line of scrimmage, and moved the goalposts back to the goal line, placing an additional premium on a good field goal kicker.

11. Dallas–Green Bay in 1967, with the temperature at 13° below zero, was the coldest ever for a pro game in the "lower forty-eight states," but in 1949 Ladd Field played the University of Alaska at Fairbanks on New Year's Day. When the temperature rose to 25° below, the players decided to junk their parkas and play in their uniforms only. The field was marked with stripes of coal dust on the snow.

12. The "Foolish Club" was the name given to the eight original owners in the AFL as a tribute to their dim-witted efforts to pour good money down a drain. They turned out not to be so foolish after all.

13. Chicago has the only team, the Bears, to have been in the NFL from the start.

14. Three major league pro teams have gone through a season unbeaten: the Chicago Bears of 1934 and 1942, and the 1972 Miami Dolphins.

15. Second-highest total in a championship game was the Lions' fifty-nine points to fourteen for the Chicago Bears in 1954.

16. *In 1935 the Giants lost to the Detroit Lions in the snow and rain in the University of Detroit stadium. There was no protection for anyone in the open stands. Paper and notes turned into a soggy mass and were thrown away as useless after the game. The crowd was an estimated 15,000.*

17. *Green Bay is the only publicly owned team. There can't be any dividends on its profits—everything goes back into the operation.*

18. *If a quarterback attempting to pass out of his end zone hits the crossbar, the pass is incomplete and the ball is dead. In 1944 Sammy Baugh, playing for the Redskins, hit the bar and the Cleveland Rams recovered for the safety, which meant the NFL title. Sammy wasn't aiming at the crossbar; the wind blowing off Lake Erie carried the ball there.*

19. *Tommy McDonald, an acrobatic pass-catching end, was the last man to play without a face mask. He spent most of his career with the Philadelphia Eagles but came back in 1968 to finish with the Cleveland Browns.*

20. *The Los Angeles Rams were the first to show up with fancy decorated helmets. Up to that time, helmets were of a basic color, with maybe a stripe. Embellishing the helmets was a summer-long job by Fred Gehrke, a Rams running back, now general manager of the Denver club. He did the job entirely by hand in his garage and didn't charge for it. Now the Cleveland Browns are the only pro team that doesn't bother with helmet adornment.*

21. *Denver defeated Detroit in the first game played between the American and National Football Leagues in 1967. It was preseason, of course.*

22. *Coaching from the bench was legalized in 1944. Before that it brought a 15-yard penalty.*

23. *A "drive-train" injury involves the leg, starting with the big toe, pushing off, and going all the way up through the foot, ankle, calf, knee, and thigh.*

24. *The football scouting combines are BLESTO, UNITED, and QUADRA. Information is provided to subscribing members on computer printouts.*

25. *The Raiders are the only team that has resisted all efforts to have them join one of the scouting combines.*

26. *With everyone getting virtually the same information, the individual club then has to decide which players it wants to follow up with more detailed viewing by its own talent people.*

27. *The first college team to use the two-platoon system was Michigan, in 1945 under Fritz Crisler. He limited the coming-and-going to his offensive and defensive lines.*

28. *The worst beating occurring in a college game involving major opponents was a 100–6 job by Houston over Tulsa in 1968.*

29. *The college record for ties in a single season is four, shared by the 1939 U.C.L.A. team and the 1937 Temple University eleven. Additionally, Temple's were all scoreless jobs.*

30. *The highest tied score between major opponents was 37–37, in the game between Alabama and Florida in 1967.*

31. *Green Bay gained 385 yards rushing vs. Philadelphia in 1978, but lost 10–3.*

32. *Miami of Ohio. An astonishing parade of top coaches have come from this relatively small university, including Red Blaik, Paul Brown, Weeb Ewbank, and Bo Schembechler.*

33. *Numbers on football jerseys were introduced in 1908 by Washington & Jefferson in a game with the University of Pittsburgh.*

34. *Scooter McLean kicked the last succesful drop-kick extra point for the Chicago Bears against the New York Giants in 1941. There's no record of the last drop-kick field goal.*

35. *The "rotator cuff" is a portion of the shoulder that prevents the arm from slipping out of its socket. A tear of the cuff obviously is a serious matter.*

36. *Bob Irsay, owner of the Colts, came into football in an unusual manner. He purchased the Los Angeles Rams from the estate of Dan Reeves, then traded the franchise to Baltimore, giving the late Carroll Rosenbloom access to the Hollywood he vastly preferred to staid Baltimore. There was also a little hipper-dipper involved with the tax problem—not to beat it, just to put off the payments.*

37. *The ill-fated World Football League played its only championship game in Birmingham with the home team beating Florida. There were a lot of rubber paychecks in the league toward the end, but the best part was the sheriff with a lien waiting to pick up the uniforms after the title game.*

38. *When the pros instituted the numbering system, allowance was made for anyone who has sported an unusual number before the rule went into effect. Anyone coming in now, however, has to conform.*

39. *The complaint against artificial turf, at least from the players and the medics, is that it doesn't cut down on injuries but inflicts a different kind. There is less "give" in artificial turf, so increased pressure is placed on the various muscles and joints of the leg. And a skin burn sustained on artificial turf can take twice as long to heal as one from grass. You can get the water off the stuff a lot faster after a downpour, though, and on a wet day you don't have to worry about wiping the mud from your eyes.*

40. *In 1951 the mercurial 25-percent owner of the Washington Redskins, Harry Wismer, fired Herman Ball, the head coach, three games into the season and announced that Heartley (Hunk) Anderson, a Chicago Bears assistant and master strategist, was joining the club in Detroit for the next day's game. Anderson showed up, but at the same time a phone call came from George Halas, the Bears' owner, saying that if they wanted to grab one of his assistants he wanted one of Washington's better tackles in return. Washington couldn't get Anderson for nothing. So Anderson went back to Chicago, and Washington assistant coach Dick Todd, a former All-Star player, finished up the season. He won more games than he lost for the rest of the season and was bounced at the end. Total time for three head coaches, twenty hours—a league record.*

41. *First coast-to-coast radio broadcast of a pro football game was the 1940 championship play-off in which the Bears beat the Redskins, 72–0. Mutual paid $2,500 for the rights. Depending on your point of view, it got either the best or the worst bargain in the history of sports.*

Index